5.oo

T

SCOTTO
More Than a Diva

SCOTTO
More Than a Diva

Renata Scotto and Octavio Roca

DOUBLEDAY & COMPANY, INC.
GARDEN CITY, NEW YORK
1984

DESIGNED BY LAURENCE ALEXANDER

Library of Congress Cataloging in Publication Data

Scotto, Renata, 1934–
Scotto: more than a diva.

Includes index.
1. Scotto, Renata, 1934– . 2. Singers—Italy—
Biography. I. Roca, Octavio, 1949– . II. Title.
ML420.S435A3   1984   782.1′092′4 [B]   82-45305
ISBN 0-385-18039-X

for Lorenzo,
for Laura and Filippo,
and for Luis

———

Contents

Foreword

By Plácido Domingo

FOREWORD

I have worked with many of the world's great sopranos, and among them all Renata Scotto occupies a very special place for all the beautiful productions and recordings we have shared.

It was in 1965 that I first heard her, in the season of her Metropolitan Opera debut as Puccini's Madama Butterfly. I remember her enormous talent soaring in that matinee broadcast, but of course she was considered more of a lyric soprano in those days. Cio-Cio-San was the most dramatic role in her repertory then, and the public had not yet discovered the versatility of this artist. Later, in 1970, we came to know each other in Verona. It was an interesting season: Renata and Carlo Bergonzi were appearing in Verdi's *La Traviata;* there was Franco Corelli as Don José in Bizet's *Carmen;* and I was singing opposite Magda Olivero in Puccini's *Manon Lescaut.* All of this was still before Renata's transformation into the artist she is today. We have learned, you see, that singing—even singing very well—is not enough.

Opera for us is a total theatrical experience. One of the most fascinating things abut Renata's career has been her complete acceptance of this maxim. Today we work for a public that has learned to appreciate and expects not only great singing but also the totality of music and drama, except for occasional extraordinary voices.

After our meeting in Verona, we sang together in New York. Our first *Faust* and our first *Vespri siciliani* at the Met were truly magical moments in both our careers. The electricity of the performances, the magnetism we felt on stage and in the house are all still vivid memories. From that time on Renata and I realized how much we had in common. We both believe in a complete absorption in the operatic characters. That is, we make singing an opera an experience that is not only vocal but scenic. We take great pleasure in what we do.

Renata Scotto is a musician. She is a studious woman who is devoted to her career. I have seen her at work and her dedication to opera is complete, profound, and remarkable. She will finish singing only to return to the score and study again. She has given herself to opera, body and soul; and she never stops learning. That is why her characterizations are always so fresh.

Does she have a temperament? Of course, but it is always reasonable, and I say this from experience. We have worked together in perfect harmony. On stage and on records we have obtained immense satisfaction from our work together. My favorite couple of all the people we have been are perhaps Manon and Des Grieux in Puccini's *Manon Lescaut*, in that beautiful production the Met mounted for us in 1980. But there are so many more, like the extraordinary *Luisa Miller* at the Met, *Adriana Lecouvreur*, *Norma*, *Tosca*. As I write these lines Renata and I are preparing and exploring Zandonai's doomed lovers in *Francesca da Rimini*. And there are our many records together, especially our album of duets, and Puccini's *Le Villi*, *Madama Butterfly*, and *Il Tabarro*; Cilèa's *Adriana Lecouvreur*, Giordano's *Andrea Chénier*, and of course Verdi's *Otello*.

The days of the diva or divo are past, and Renata Scotto is more than a diva. In today's opera world, with the greatly expanded media attention and the ever-growing public, *divismo* has all but disappeared. Today's opera

F O R E W O R D

star is a social phenomenon of a different nature, a singer who gives everything to his or her public.

As for vocal categories, Renata has ignored them with spectacular success. I can sympathize with her efforts. Once upon a time Gigli, Martinelli, Caruso, Fleta all were tenors who sang the tenor repertory. There was nobody telling them "This is too dramatic for you," or "You are only a lyric." From Don Ottavio to Otello, from Alfredo Germont to Lohengrin, there were simply tenor roles to be sung by tenors. What mattered to them, and what matters to us today, is to know oneself, what one can sing, and to sing it well. That is all. The real artist knows his talent.

A singer's biography can be an incomplete thing. After all, the true story is in the singing, not in the writing. I know, I have written a book myself. The readers will find much pleasure in this book, for a singer's life still holds a certain fascination. There is much to learn from this story, many secrets to a great career, intricacies of vocal technique, acting, touching the hearts of an audience. There is much to learn here about life.

New York, 1984

SCOTTO
More Than a Diva

One

Growing Up to Violetta

S C O T T O

My hometown has changed so much. Sometimes when I go home to Savona I have trouble recognizing the old neighborhoods of this Ligurian fishing town where I was born on February 24, 1934. It is the largest city on the Italian Riviera after Genoa, and today it looks it. Taller buildings have replaced the ones that bombs destroyed forty years ago; a large factory makes little cars and employs countless men who used to fish for a living; more than 75,000 people live here. The Via Paleocapa still cuts the city in half and leads to the port, and it was around this same port that the Savonese built their city. Near here the severe stones of the Fortress of Priamar recall older wars; near here the cathedral was built with gifts from Pope Julius II on the site of an earlier and now lost church. Two stone lions used to guard the entrance, but they were taken away by the plundering Genoese and now guard their church. Once fifty towers protected Savona, now there is only the old Tower of Brandale left to look on her history. To the north are mountains I would get to know well; to the east is the beach of Albissola, where I would be married. Past the old Palazzo Pozzobonello, which was almost razed by American bombs in the war but is now an art museum, are neighborhoods for working classes. Here is where my family lived. My mother Santina, nicknamed Silvia, was a seamstress who was fond of saying that life is like a bread made of many crusts: some are harder and some are soft, and all are nourishing. She never complained, not even during the war, and she taught me to smile and smile again in the face of

3

every trial. My father Giuseppe was a policeman, and everyone called him Gino.

I remember that before the war, when I was very little, there was much talk about Mussolini and discipline, about the virtues of sports and study, about pomp and marches; it all sounded very exciting. My older sister Luciana was made to join the Piccole Italiane and wore the Fascist uniform to school. I threw a tantrum because I wanted to have a uniform just like hers; I was too young to go to school so of course, I could not join yet. Finally my mother made me a uniform like my sister's. I was so proud of my costume, I ran around in it, I sang in it.

When the war began Savona was a dangerous place to be, since it was an important port and all harbors were in danger of being bombed. So my father sent my mother and his two girls north to Tovo San Giacomo, in the Ligurian Alps; somehow Mamma managed to leave my Young Fascist uniform behind.

My father had to stay in Savona. Once a month, on Sunday, he would walk up to see us and would bring what food and gifts he could; sometimes he brought meat. The rest of the time we were alone, and it was not easy. One time my father did not come on Sunday, or the next Sunday, and no one expected to see him alive again. How my mother cried for joy when he turned up at the door. He managed to get us a goat, and eventually we also had some chickens, so now we children could have milk and eggs and my mother could make cheese and butter. We raised some vegetables in a little garden. And Mother made pasta. Pasta. People think Italians eat so well, they have this image of how much we adore pasta, how delicious, fabulous, even chic pasta is. The reason we ate so much pasta was simple: it hurts to have an empty stomach, and with pasta it is easy to feel full and not to hurt anymore; pasta is cheap and keeps away hunger pains, it is a necessity. It is a taste cultivated in scarcity.

My mother worked all day sewing and would hope to keep her hands warm enough in winter to be able to go on using them. One day I would sing of a seamstress like my mother, and I would understand Mimi's sweet desperation and her happiness by remembering Santina the seamstress as she worked and sang.

It was here in Tovo San Giacomo that I began school, with no books and not much to eat. But I have to say that it is only now that I see how difficult it all was. My mother made it easy, we children did not notice that anything was wrong. It was a happy time, really; I was free, I sang all the time, I ate lunch at the window, we all loved each other so much. Everybody in the village knew me as the singer, and I would learn the latest Beniamino Gigli songs, like "Mamma," and offer them from our window. The villagers applauded; sometimes they gave me candy so I would sing an encore and I was always ready to sing another song.

We lived in two rooms that were even smaller than the two rooms we had had in Savona; the kitchen had a fireplace, the floor was unfinished, and the toilet was outside. My mother's dreams were simple: to have a mirror, to grow a few vegetables and raise chickens, to sew enough to trade for more food for us; and to see the end of the war. We had friends who managed to bake bread, and my mother sewed for them in return for loaves twice a week.

A child sees things quite clearly, I am convinced; then she ignores what she sees. That is how children can get used to anything and how they remember everything. I did, and I do. We were almost starving and always in danger, but I was happy then. Only now when I recall my mother do I recognize the terror that she kept from her girls. Small, humble Santina, afraid and strong, with her tenacity and her fears, her horrible fears that we would not have enough to eat, that some Sunday Gino might not come. "Go see if you can see your father coming." She would send us to the hills while she stayed behind and prayed: "Madonna, let Gino be alive, let Gino be alive." She made a living sewing, and the uniform did not matter: she sewed for passing Fascist officers, for the Nazis, for the Americans. Sometimes uniforms were left behind, and when the blood could be boiled away she would cut them up to make clothes for me and Luciana. I remember how I played most often in a favorite pair of trousers made from khaki camouflage material. Soon I learned to sew them myself and helped mother, especially in winter when her hands chapped as she sewed in the cold all day.

Those were important days, hard days for Italy; but looking back on the war now, I doubt that anyone in Tovo San Giacomo had a sense of history. We had a sense of survival. We had been poor in normal times, and the war only made us poorer. By the second year my sister Luciana and I played a macabre game of running to the hills and guessing where the bombs would fall: the American planes had to swoop in formation over our village on their way to bomb Savona, Albissola, and Vado Ligure; we could guess by their whistled glissandi where the bombs would fall, so we would count and bet, perched high on mountains, imagining where they hit. The planes came every day, even as the uniforms of the soldiers who passed through town changed colors.

After the last army left we returned to Savona for the first time in four years. We were fortunate that our apartment still stood, even if amid rubble; and we returned to live there near the sea when the war ended. My father had not been hurt, and he was still a policeman.

Our apartment was in a stubby building, overlooking a courtyard, not far from where the fishermen met. The balcony off the kitchen was the largest place to play, and here I sang out when I was free, with my mother watching and smiling on cool summer afternoons. I would hold on to the iron rail and sing popular songs, and again the neighbors applauded and gave me candy. You see, I never sang for nothing in my life. Soon I had to earn more than candy, and by the age of ten I was helping my mother with her sewing after school.

The most fun I had was always with my uncle Salvatore, a fisherman from Carlo Forte, Sardinia, who married my mother's sister. He was a great, rough man who loved children and had none of his own; and I was his favorite. When I was about nine or ten he took me fishing with him, against my mother's cries and wringing of hands. I remember we left the house at dawn, and how fascinated he was with what he called the silent conversation with the fish and the sea, how he would let me join in by singing and how he himself would sing. It was always song and talk of song, and he seemed to take his little niece seriously. He was not very educated, but he knew songs of Verdi, Mascagni, Puccini, and Tosti, and I would teach him any new popular tunes I had learned in town. It is one of my sweetest memories.

I remember my uncle sitting in front of a huge mountain of spaghetti that he had cooked himself, at the beach house in Albissola where he fished. He was so big, he would hug all of us at the same time, my cousins Albertina and Anna Maria and me. After the war we really grew up on that beach, especially in summers. All three of us could go fishing with Uncle Salvatore as long as we didn't touch anything. He taught me to swim. Today I have a pool, a very beautiful place to swim; and I can travel to any beach I like. But I don't think it will ever be like swimming in the Mediterranean off my uncle's boat as he fished. I see my children today, I see how I must thank God that they have everything; yet I still wish for them some of that happiness that I knew even in poverty: I had nothing, but I sang and I was always happy.

There was not much going on as a rule at the Teatro Chiabrera in Savona, but for Christmas every year there was a little opera season for two weeks. "Renata, I think you'll like the opera," announced Uncle Salvatore to his twelve-year-old niece. I had never seen opera, of course; I only knew the word from my uncle. Now I would be taken to see Verdi's *Rigoletto* with the great Tito Gobbi as the tormented hunchback.

My uncle told me the story before going to the theater, and I remember thinking, "How can a hunchback sing all that, how is he going to move like that?" Then the curtain went up that Christmas Eve. I had never seen anything so beautiful in my life. So much passion, a daughter's love for her father and later for a treacherous young man, her sacrifice, her transformation, the father's tragedy. And all of it was *sung*, it was told in music that was as Italian and as familiar to me as anything I sang in my uncle's boat, but it was so much more beautiful, so easy to love, and so well aimed at the heart.

And most of all there was Tito Gobbi. I could not believe how that voice filled the theater, how it rang and thrilled; to this day I can hear *"Cortigiani, vil razza"* only in his voice, I know just how it sounded that night at the Chiabrera. Gobbi the great singer and Gobbi the great actor made me decide that night that I would be an opera singer. I fell in love with opera, that was all I could talk about.

I went home and made a hump out of a cushion and ran around the apartment cursing the courtiers—it never occurred to me to want to play Gilda then. Years later I would play Gilda to Gobbi's Rigoletto, and it would be one of my happiest moments onstage. And even now, when I receive letters from young people who tell me that I may have inspired them to sing, I remember how Gobbi inspired me, how he made me want to sing, and I feel very much part of a beautiful cycle. There is of course an ugly side to the artistic struggles of young singers, and for many without enough talent it can be a frustrating life; but for the few who have the talent, that inspiration, that model, can be the key to finding their vocation and their worth. Gobbi was that inspiration for me when I was twelve years old.

My mother and father bought me an upright piano, with Uncle Salvatore's help, for forty-five thousand lire; in a home where I still shared a bed with my sister and there was little furniture, it was a sacrifice for which I was profoundly happy and grateful, and I took my music seriously from that moment on.

My first audition, and a very important one, came in 1948. My father's cousin Frank Baglietto lived in America. He still does, actually; he lives in New Rochelle not far from me today. Anyway, he was our American cousin, and he was to visit the family that summer.

Imagine, to an Italian girl, provincial, young, never having been out of Savona except to hide out in the hills during the war—just imagine what a cousin from America meant in those days. To have a relative who actually lived somewhere over the rainbow in that combination of Hollywood and heaven we believed New York to be was beyond my imagination. So when my father suggested that I audition for Cousin Frank, I prepared my program very carefully. It would be the first time that I had sung for anyone other than immediate family or neighbors.

The day of Frank's arrival we introduced him to my piano teacher—Barbagelatta she was called—who was to accompany me. I put on my only white linen dress, my best, with a single blue ribbon around the bodice and Mother's ruffles at the sleeves. I felt pretty, made my entrance from the bedroom, and sang Verdi's *"Stride la vampa!"* for my cousin. He listened carefully, then everyone waited for him to give his opinion. He was very sweet and encouraging and told me that I had a beautiful voice. Then he said, "Perhaps one day you can come to America." I will never forget that.

My next trip was a little closer to home, actually. When I was fourteen my uncle and aunt took me to Milan for an audition with a famous maestro. I thought I was a mezzo and I had learned *"Stride la vampa!"* which I sang with what I thought was dramatic conviction. The maestro listened carefully and smiled, then he took my aunt aside and told her, "She has a voice, but for God's sake let her go back to playing with dolls for a while." Then he turned to me and asked me to come back in two years. I would, of course; I had to go to Milan if I really wanted to sing. Milan meant La Scala, great singers, conductors, directors; great opera. The possibilities after the war were all there, and there I had to be.

My mother of course could not afford to put me up there, but with family help a convent of Canossian nuns was found where I could live and work and where I could be near my teacher for the music lessons I so much wanted. My sister Luciana, five years older, was working as a saleswoman in a dry goods store in Savona, and she gave me the money for the trip; she did that, at what I know was a great sacrifice each time I traveled between Savona and Milan. I will always love her very much for having done that. For the next four years I worked and studied with the nuns and lived in the convent, returning home to Savona only in the summer and Christmas to sing to my family what I had learned.

I showed up at the convent with two musical scores, gifts from my mother: Verdi's *La Traviata* and Puccini's *Manon Lescaut*. The nuns were not pleased with this teen-ager who brought with her tales of two fallen women, especially the one about the girl who was lost on her way to the convent! After some struggle I managed to keep the scores, although it was not easy.

Life at the convent was simple. By seven each morning I was ready in my brown cotton uniform to attend the first class, and I would go from lesson to lesson until three in the afternoon, when I would work until dinnertime. Mother had taught me to sew well, and soon I was doing all the sewing for the good sisters. On Sundays they would let me sing in church, usually one Ave Maria or another to organ accompaniment.

The convent was near the Duomo, which I got to know well, and fifteen minutes from my voice teacher, the old baritone Emilio Ghirardini, to whom I added Professor Merlini a year later. Arnaldo Bassi was my piano teacher. It was not a time for auditions but one for study and for work.

Being in Milan was in itself more exciting than anything in my previous experience. It is Italy's second largest city, but it was the most formidable to me, the center of the world for a singer. I will never forget entering La Scala for the first time, being greeted by the statues of the men who would become so important in my life: Rossini, Bellini, Donizetti, Verdi. I remember feeling at home here and putting up with anything at the convent just to be able to remain in Milan and study.

There was one nun, Suor Maria, who hated me and kept trying to take away my music scores. She once had me sent up before Mother Superior, herself no music lover, who gave me for the first of many times a lecture on how "music is not important in life, Renata; you have to concentrate more on your work and your studies, you have to pray. You might make a good nun one day." "No, thank you," I thought; but I kept quiet and did my best. I am sure that I was not a very good student, since it really was only music that filled my head then. But my work was good.

One young nun, Suor Teresa, became my friend, and though our friendship made the dreaded Suor Maria jealous, I felt less lonely. Suor Teresa liked music and helped me with the piano. It was she who suggested that I sing in church Sunday mornings and it was thanks to this that I was able to keep my scores of *Manon Lescaut* and *La Traviata* when Suor Maria tried to take them away; I needed my scores so I could study and sing better in church.

We were allowed to talk to our parents only once a

month. There was a *parlatorio* where visitors were allowed to speak to us, but we could barely touch each other. So on visiting days I would sit in front of my mother and sister and just talk to them. I had to obey the rules, but most of the time I was lonely and I missed being hugged by my mother very much. Still, my biggest fear was that I would break one of the convent rules and have to return to Savona. Our mail was always opened before it reached us. Today the thought outrages me, but I did not give it much thought then. Only once, perhaps. Over the summer I had met a boy on the beach in Albissola. We were both sixteen. He wrote me at the convent and I had to read the letter, already opened, in Mother Superior's office. I felt very humiliated and hurt. "Who is this boy? Why is he writing to you?" I explained that he was a friend from home, just a friend. "Tell him not to write to you anymore. Here, write the letter now." I obeyed.

Years later I was again in a convent, this time on stage at the Metropolitan Opera in New York. The cold severity of Puccini's refectory was out of my past, you see, not just out of the libretto. As Suor Angelica met with her aunt I recalled how much I wanted to touch my mother all those times she visited, how I wanted her to stay, how I obeyed. I remembered the loneliness of obedience. I had to re-create for Puccini's opera the delicate naiveté of a young nun's pain and I drew upon many memories of my days with the good Canossian sisters.

After a while I began to audition. First I sang in a very low voice, and I am almost horrified to remember what I did to my voice in those days. I would open with Giuseppe Giordani's Neapolitan song *"Caro mio ben, credimi almen."* Then I would sing a song or short aria that I was studying at the time, usually Ponchielli's *"A te questo*

rosario" from *La Gioconda*. And I would close with my
pièce de résistance, Verdi's *"Stride la vampa!"* which had
impressed my cousin Frank so well. I had little idea what
the music was about, but I sang out.

I did begin to have suspicions about my being a
mezzo-soprano; perhaps I was a soprano. Maestro
Ghirardini was not sure, so he decided to put my voice to
the test. After a few months of study I gave my first recital
in Piacenza, joining three other students with Emilio
Ghirardini at the piano. I sang both soprano music and
mezzo-soprano music: Verdi's *"O cieli azzurri"* and *"Stride
la vampa!"* We would decide in recital which sounded better and which was better received. It was November 3,
1950. My first review, the next day in the *Corriere di Piacenza*, said that "Young Signorina Scotto, a teenager from
Savona who has studied for only three months, struck us
with an abundance of vocal power which, if carefully nur-
tured, should lead to a very bright future as a soprano."
So, with that recital, I decided that I would be a soprano.

After the concert, of course, I returned to the convent
to live and work. On every Sunday we were allowed to go
out, and my choice was always La Scala. I had no money
for tickets, but Maestro Arnaldo Bassi had an *abbonamento*,
a subscription, which gave him passes for standing room,
and these he gave me for Sunday matinees. Each Sunday
after church I would join the stampede of standees rush-
ing for the best unnumbered places in the *loggione*. I only
had until five o'clock or else the nuns would not let me out
the following week, so I had to be careful to leave before
five no matter how long the opera was. But even if I never
did see the endings of *Die Meistersinger* or *La Gioconda*, it
was like heaven when I did catch Stignani and Callas, Di
Stefano, or Schwarzkopf, or the great conductors like

Furtwängler or Votto. I was only sorry when La Scala had a ballet for the matinee, not because I dislike ballet but because it meant that I would have to wait another week to see an opera.

With my teacher Ghirardini, eventually I began to think of myself as a soprano, and I auditioned as a soprano. I remember the first important one was for the RAI network, but both I and an older girl named Anita Cerquetti were eliminated in the finals. At least now I was beginning to look my age; I remember that when I had that first audition, accompanied by my young aunt, the maestri could not believe that it was this child who wanted to sing and asked several times if my aunt was sure that I was the singer.

Then in 1952 Ghirardini encouraged me to enter the competition of the Milan Lyric Association. It was an important and useful contest, not only for the prestige but also because the winner earned more than a medal or even money. The prize was a performance, an operatic debut in a role to be chosen after the competition and to be sung at the Teatro Nuovo in Milan.

I had entered the same competition the year before but had been eliminated before the finals. In the process I learned a lesson that was good for a young singer. That first time I sang Suzel's sweet *"Son pochi fiori"* from Mascagni's opera *L'amico Fritz*. I thought I sang it very well, and I did not realize what a poor choice that simple song is for an audition. I was crushed.

I still hoped for everything, though, and hope breeds and liberates its own kind of strength. At seventeen I was naive, not very well educated, and still very poor, sewing and cleaning for the nuns at the Canossian convent, earning my keep and my lessons and my Sunday out for the opera. But I was a fast learner and I was strong. In Italy auditions are less common than they are in the United States, or at least they were in those days. It was a small musical world and when a voice was good the word got around. One usually auditioned only for a commercial agent or for an important competition. This was an important competition, and this time I decided to choose something to sing that would really tell them something about Renata Scotto's voice.

There were a thousand applicants, then there were five hundred, and finally ten finalists of which I was one. The three judges for the final rounds were Cesare Giulio Paribeni, Renzo Bianchi, and the music critic Eugenio Gara. Throughout the competition I had been singing the Jewel Song from Gounod's *Faust* and *"È strano. . . . Sempre libera"* from *La Traviata*, with Ghirardini accompanying me. When I stepped onstage for the finals I was asked what I would sing. I answered, "Verdi, *La Traviata*, Violetta's aria from Act I." I sang very well, and I won the competition and the title role in *La Traviata* for the Teatro Nuovo's opening night of the season. A good friend who made it to the final rounds, the bass Paolo Washington, was given a role later that season as well.

So there I was, never having been on the operatic stage before and set to open a season in Milan with one of the most difficult and beautiful roles I would ever sing. It was a lucky choice, for as I would later learn Verdi's music lifts the libretto of *Traviata* to the heavens; and although it would take me years to learn who Violetta is, singing the music would be enough for success in the beginning. If I sang very well.

Of course I needed to prepare. I left the convent to go back to Savona with the good news, and my uncle Salvatore, who had been ill, gathered up a young man's energy, cornered a local impresario at the Teatro Chiabrera, and convinced him to let me sing Violetta in Savona, for no money—not even the chocolate candy this same man used to give me when I was little—as a preparation for the Milan opening. This was to be in the same theater where I had fallen in love with opera, my first theater. Years later most people would know about my debut in Milan as Violetta, my official debut in opera. But very few know of this unofficial *Traviata*, which really was my first. It was in Savona that I broke the ice and learned to establish a bond with the public. And what a public! The house was sold out for that Christmas Eve of 1952, half coming to wish well to the policeman's daughter they all knew, the others with a curiosity and not much hope for this eighteen-year-old girl who dared to play Verdi's heroine. There were friends and there were those who demanded proof of my talent; and the best in the audience could fit in both categories. I knew what this meant to me, that this and the Milan performance were my big chance and that if I failed I would retire to Savona for good, to an anonymous future as a housewife, to settle down. I was young and I wanted more, I wanted to sing more than anything else in the world. So I did.

It was the most beautiful Christmas of my life, certainly the sweetest. In the first theater I had ever visited I sang the opera that I would sing most often in my career.

Nello Romani sang Alfredo, Giuseppe Manacchini sang his father, my friend Maria Teresa Bertasi doubled as Flora and Annina, with the Chiabrera's Maestro Pessina conducting. There was very little rehearsal but the energy carried us through, and the evening was a big success. The critic of *L'Unità* was representative of the reviews when he wrote on December 27 that "Scotto earned an unreserved success. . . . She has returned to her native town for her debut, a proof of her courage as much as her considerable talent. And Savona has acclaimed her in triumph. From her entrance she showed authority and total command of the stage, with measured gestures and a most fresh vocal timbre . . . justifying the public's delirium after her *'Amami, Alfredo.'*"

My gestures were measured, actually, because I really did not know what to do; the stage direction had consisted mostly of the "Come here, move there, exit left" variety, and I did not know the character at all. I began to learn that night that the public could be kind but that it deserved better; and soon I would study and study again and again this brilliant music drama.

The Milan opening was set for Thursday, July 2, 1953. This coincided with the closing of La Scala, and much of the same public went to the experimental Teatro Nuovo. There was much publicity about this competition winner's debut, and the house was sold out a month in advance, with many important people attending.

My nerves, as always, lasted only until the minute I stepped onstage. Then I felt at home. I will always be especially happy that my uncle Salvatore was there that night. He was already ill, and he soon died; he would never hear me sing in all the important theaters he had dreamed for me. But he was there for my debut, he was my biggest fan, so proud of his niece. For him, for my family, and for myself, I walked from the wings into Violetta's frantic party. I greeted my guests and was introduced to a young man, Alfredo, who apparently had admired this poor courtesan for some time. I asked him for a drinking song, which he gave center stage with eyes fixed on the conductor, then I and the guests joined in. I was in a daze, I felt ill, the young man helped me and confessed his love. I tried to warn him that such sincerity was dangerous, but he persisted; so I took a flower from my breast and asked him to return as it began to fade. The guests started to leave, and the desperate frolics ended, leaving me alone onstage wondering if it was worth trusting this new feeling. This was the same scene with which I had won the audition, of course, and now I sang it in context.

To break the dictates of tradition, one should act from experience and intelligence, not from ignorance and instinct. I would break many rules soon enough, but not yet. I had a tradition to follow, did it well, and the public liked it very much; it takes experience to know when and how to challenge tradition, and this was not the time. So I began *"È strano, è strano . . ."* as a musical recitation and hoped that the music would be enough; I recalled dreams of young love and imagined real happiness as Violetta, interpolating many details that Verdi did not write but which were expected and frankly very exciting, like larcenous rubati in the cavatina and a long and ringing E-flat at the end of *"Sempre libera."* As Verdi's Violetta denounced the folly of love and promised herself to live out her days in pleasure, the curtain came down to the loudest applause I had ever heard.

In Act II Violetta and Alfredo are living together and he sings of the pleasures of life with his lover; when he finds out that Violetta has been selling her possessions in order to support their life away from Paris, he returns to the city to set matters right. At that point Alfredo's father pays a surprise visit, and Violetta's inevitable doom is clear. I remember little of the evening, actually—I was in another world for the first time. But I remember that in

"Dite alla giovine," as Violetta agrees to give up the love of her life, I was in tears and so were many in the theater; I remember that the music transported me in the short, breathless phrases that Violetta nervously showers on Alfredo before begging him to love her; and I remember that phrase, *"Amami, Alfredo,"* as one of the most touching lines I would ever sing. My voice did everything I wanted it to do, and it seemed to get more powerful as the evening wore on. In *"Addio del passato"* I did not add any notes, although the beat was very free, and the high A that floats in resignation ended not when Scotto's breath ended but when Violetta could no longer sing. I could hear life leaving the voice at that moment. I had had no acting lessons but somehow, instinctively, I remember that when I knelt in rage at death and when I rose to my lover's arms for one final moment I was not myself. I was Violetta.

It was a triumph, and I knew that I would be sharing many years with the public. What followed were some very happy years, easy years even. That night I made some friends and some fans.

The great tenor Beniamino Gigli, whose songs I had learned from the radio and sung my whole life, asked me to join him in a concert! And so I did, in Pesaro, singing the Jewel Song from *Faust*, two songs, and even joining the great Gigli in the Cherry Duet from Mascagni's *L'amico Fritz*. It was heaven, it was fantastic.

Also present at that first *Traviata* in Milan was the soprano Mafalda Favero. She came backstage—it was such a new feeling to hear people who were not family tell me how well I had sung—and congratulated me. Favero had been the great Adriana Lecouvreur of the previous generation, a singer I admired very much from records although I never saw her onstage; she was known to be a great singing actress. Her encouragement that night was generous and beautiful, and I was especially pleased when she volunteered in a newspaper interview that, "in this young woman, art is second nature."

The offers to sing came, and suddenly it seemed as if I would have a recital every other week. I was offered *Madama Butterfly* by Puccini for a special gala performance at the Chiabrera, and Mafalda Favero's generosity became apparent once more. Coaching for such a role was beyond the abilities of Maestro Ghirardini, and Mafalda came to his studio to work with me on preparing Cio-Cio-San. She showed great patience and enthusiasm working with this teenage soprano who she insisted was so much like her. I remember that she taught me how to move my hands, how to sing dramatic lines without forcing either the voice or the body.

"Be careful, Renata. The role is a voice killer," she would caution. "Remember that you have to know your strength and that you can't waste any of it because you will need it all to say farewell to your child and to your life in the last act." She gave me some excellent advice; much of it I like to pass on to young singers today.

I sang my first *Butterfly* in Savona, and this time they not only applauded but they also paid me twenty-five thousand lire, not quite the thirty thousand I had received for the Milan *Traviata*, but not bad; from that night on, I could send some money home to my family.

I had success with Puccini's Japanese heroine from the beginning, and I repeated the role as my debut in the Teatro Pergolesi and other small houses. It was my debut role on October 10 at La Fenice in Venice, that most magical of cities. I stayed in Venice for Mascagni's *L'amico Fritz* the following day, finally singing all of this story of the young Jewish girl Suzel and her sweet romance with a shy and older gentleman.

To sing in the city of Monteverdi and Vivaldi and to travel to such exquisite surroundings was all very dangerous and exciting. Exciting of course because I was still living at the convent and I simply had not had a very complicated life before; I had never dreamed that I would have such a frantic success so soon, and that I would be singing in the great theaters in the year of my debut. Dangerous because my technique was not right and I was singing on borrowed time until I could correct it. A teacher and coach is so important for a singer, and Ghirardini with all his good intentions was not particularly good for my development as an artist. He had a talent for explaining at length things I already knew and an equal talent for turning a deaf ear to the problems I could feel. In my case I was young and had a voice, so I used it naturally; but soon I would need help. Not until two years later would I meet Alfredo Kraus, a Spanish tenor who sang like a young Tito Schipa; he took me to his teacher, the Catalan Mercedes Llopart, who really taught me how to sing.

But I am getting ahead of the story. In this year of danger and excitement, 1953, I heard backstage at La Fenice that La Scala was mounting a new production of Catalani's *La Wally* for the opening night of the following season with some of Italy's biggest stars—Renata Tebaldi, Mario Del Monaco, and Giorgio Tozzi—in the leading roles. I heard that there might be auditions for some of the other parts. Was I ready for La Scala? There seemed to be only one way to find out.

Two

All Those Nice Girls, and Manon

Alfredo Catalani had been accused of Germanizing Italian music at a time when Verdi and Puccini were kings, but in his opera *La Wally* he created a masterpiece that despite its Northern themes beats with an Italianate heart. It was his last and his best opera, a favorite of Toscanini, who not only championed it but also named his daughter after the heroine. It is a lush musical drama of two lovers who meet their death in an avalanche in the spectacular finale; before they do, there is a boy called Walter who adds musical and dramatic color with beer-drinking charm and hair-raising coloratura. He is played by a soprano, and that is the role for which I auditioned at La Scala with Maestro Carlo Maria Giulini. The new production was to open the 1954 Scala season, and the role of Walter had not been cast.

My real studying would come soon enough, but in that first year I had little dramatic idea of the characters of Violetta, Cio-Cio-San, and all those nice girls with nice music that I was impersonating within weeks of my debut: Suzel, Micaëla, Leila, Norina. I knew that I had a voice, and I always had confidence—that was the first requirement. When success came, so did opportunity, and La Scala was the biggest opportunity of all. I did not think that I was ready for such a theater, but I knew that I could sing the role of Walter and the time to try was right then.

There were four singers ahead of me that day, and two waiting. I stepped onstage to face Carlo Maria Giulini and Victor de Sabata, Giulini's mentor and the unofficial musical director of La Scala. I sang Walter's aria, which I had prepared for the audition. The two maestri talked for a bit and I overheard De Sabata say, "Forget about the rest." Then Maestro Giulini said to me, "Thank you very much. Brava. Can you report to rehearsal on Monday?"

I showed up ready to work in chinos and a sweater and the director said, "But you are a kid!" He was very worried. He looked me over and then said that there was something wrong. "It's your nose. You'll have to change your nose, it's too small; no one will see it."

So on the first day at La Scala I heard the first of a string of suggestions, not for the last time. ("You're too short" is the most common, although who said that Walter —or Tosca or Norma for that matter—has to be an Amazon no one has ever explained to me.) At any rate, I was told that I would have to wear a plastic nose for the production. Fine, I said. So I wore a plastic nose the first night, and afterward I realized it was not the nose they were applauding.

The rehearsals went well after that day, and the act of walking onto the stage of La Scala gave me a thrill each time. I was still living in Milan at the convent, incidentally; the atmosphere was still somewhere between a jail and a very austere kindergarten. But it was, after all, the first place where I had had a bed to myself and I was in no hurry to leave.

I remember one day standing by the stage door waiting for the rain to stop so I could run to the tram, when I heard this voice calling my name from a fabulous American car; it was shiny and huge, the kind we did not see very often in Italy in those days. It slowed down in front of me and it turned out to be Mario Del Monaco driving this throne on wheels.

"You're soaked, you'll never catch a taxi here!" he said, opening the door.

"You must be kidding," I replied. I don't think I had

ever taken a taxi in Milan; I either took the tram or walked. At the moment La Scala had me on a modest monthly stipend, and I would be paid by the performance when the performances began. Whatever little money I had left, I sent home.

"Your car is like a dream, Mario. I have never seen anything like it."

"Would you like to drive it?"

I didn't think it would hurt to keep it from him that I had not quite learned to drive yet, so I took the wheel and received my first driving lesson from a tenor! It was fun talking to him and he wanted to prolong the ride, but I had to explain to him that the nuns were expecting me back. I must confess that I really had not discovered boys at the age of nineteen. So Mario took me home. The looks I got from the good Canossian sisters and from the other girls when I pulled up in front of the convent!

Mario became a friend that day; he said some very nice things about my singing and that the rehearsal was going very well, and then he told me as I got out of the car, ". . . and don't worry, Renata, one day you too will have a car like this one."

La Wally opened on December 7, 1954. The success was fabulous, and in all modesty I have to say that I was surprised and thrilled to read the newspaper reports that, while Tebaldi and Del Monaco got seven curtain calls each, I was called back for fifteen. Facing the audience from Italy's greatest stage and being asked to return again and again for applause were almost too much for that young girl. I felt that I had a home.

After the Scala Walter, I decided to move to my own apartment, and the papers were very dear about the move;

a picture of me cooking pasta in my new kitchen even appeared in the *Corriere della Sera.*

The next few years were full of offers, some very good, others not. La Scala wanted me back, but the roles were not right; I thought that it was wonderful to have had such success with the role of Walter in that great house, but I also thought that if I were to have a great career I had to return in a protagonist's role, and this La Scala could not offer yet. They were right, of course, since I needed the experience of many theaters before I would be able to give what one should give in the most competitive situations. The best role they could give me for the next season was that of Lisa in *La Sonnambula,* and I said no.

My friends thought I was crazy to leave La Scala. They told me again and again how difficult it was even to be a guest of the company, how lucky I was to be a member, with permanent work in the most prestigious theater in the world. "How can you even think of quitting?" they asked. But I knew that I had much to learn and that the way to learn it was not in Milan and not in smaller roles. "Leading roles in smaller theaters are better than second leads at La Scala," I would tell them. "I will be a prima donna or nothing."

So I began to get to know my country very well. Within a year the gamble seemed to be a lucky one as I made my debut in the Teatro San Carlo in Naples as Madama Butterfly. It is a great and gorgeous theater, built in 1737 and with perfect acoustics. In its gray and white bosom beauty feels at home, and from the curtain a singer can look up past the balcony to the ceiling, where on a good night Apollo and the Muses smile on the singers from a fresco on high.

It was a very good night, and I sang *Madama Butterfly* all through Italy after that. I also returned to La Fenice, a perfect theater, and got to know better its home city of Venice where the clocks count only the serene and happy hours. In Venice I sang Micaëla in Bizet's *Carmen*, which I then sang at the Rome Opera. It was Micaëla that first took me to one of the most fabulous theaters in the world, the Arena of Verona. It was very moving to sing in a theater where the voice has been heard for so many centuries. The Arena is almost as large as the Coliseum in Rome, but it is no relic; it is a living theater with incredible acoustics good enough to let twenty-five thousand be thrilled by opera each night during the summer season.

Turandot took me to Trieste, where I sang my first Liù; and I fell in love with this last of Puccini's women who is so close in spirit to his Butterfly. I sang my first Sophie in *Werther* in Rome and then returned to La Fenice for more Micaëlas, a role I also sang in many other theaters.

I did not especially want to repeat my role of Walter in *La Wally*, but I made one exception for a great occasion in Lucca, where Maria Caniglia was to be the prima donna. Hers was one of the great voices of the period before and immediately after the Second World War. I was very honored to sing with her and she later became a good friend. It was she and her husband, Maestro Pino Donati, who arranged for my American debut with the Lyric Opera of Chicago, and she was always very protective of her younger colleague, very generous.

In 1954 I auditioned for the first time for a stage director rather than a conductor. His name was Riccardo Moresco, and he was casting the lead in Gian Carlo Menotti's comedy *Amelia al ballo*. "You may sing very well, but I am not sure that you can play comedy." I think he had seen my Butterfly recently.

I began accompanying myself at the piano in the introduction to Norina's entrance aria from *Don Pasquale,* signaled the pianist to take over, and proceeded through the sexy, funny piece to sing it right to Riccardo, finishing with a turn and asking over my shoulder, "How sure are you that I can't be your Amelia?" He liked the audition, and he cast me to sing the role in the Cairo Opera House!

It was an exotic chance to leave Italy for the first time, in 1954; I went to Cairo again in 1955. There I sang Menotti's *Amelia,* followed by *La Traviata,* Bizet's *I pescatori di perle,* and *L'amico Fritz.* The public and press enjoyed the Menotti piece best, calling it a holiday from the tragic muse. I too enjoyed playing comedy quite a bit; I don't do it often enough. In Cairo too I found the score that would give me my first Mozart heroine, Donna Elvira, although it was not until the following year that with Llopart I really studied the part. Elvira is a fascinating and challenging role, much more interesting than Donna Anna; she has so much anger and compassion, all so clearly expressed in such gorgeous music.

It's a funny thing about Mozart and Italian singers. Few Italian artists are given the chance to sing Mozart's Italian masterpieces, *Don Giovanni, Così fan tutte, Le nozze di Figaro.* Some time ago there was good reason to keep the Italians away, I admit. In our century, perhaps until the 1940s Mozart, along with Bellini and Verdi, was often sung with vulgar verismo exaggerations. *Norma* sounded like *Cavalleria,* and so did *Don Giovanni.* So at some point the Germans said, "Enough!" and took over, creating what many people now call the German Mozart Style. But Mozart *a la tedesca* is as wrong as the verismo approach, because music is simply music. And often the singers who make a specialty of Mozart are so worried about creating *Kunst* that they forget to make theater. There is really no mystique or special difficulty about singing Mozart, and its importance is exaggerated by the keepers of the flame. We would be fortunate indeed if the same attention were always paid to the proper way to sing Bellini, Rossini, and Donizetti. When Mozart wrote Italian operas, despite what the Germans may say, he wrote Italian operas.

Wilhelm Furtwängler, who knew his music, chose Tito Gobbi for his Don Giovanni at Salzburg. Cesare Siepi was a great Mozart singer, and Ettore Bastianini could have been a wonderful Don Giovanni too, if only he had been given the chance. Ilva Ligabue is a great Mozartian. And above all today Mirella Freni has shown the world that it is possible and beautiful to sing Mozart in a true Italian style. Even as I write this I am preparing to return to Mozart, as Vitellia in *La Clemenza di Tito* for the 1984–85 Metropolitan Opera season. James Levine asked me to take the role and I accepted gladly.

When I first sang Mozart it was a beautiful experience, a performance that was well received, but my career was destined to move in a different direction. I sang Donna Elvira for my London debut on May 14, 1957, at the old Stoll Theater, in a season that included Adina and Violetta as well. This was also only months before my debut in *La Sonnambula,* but before recalling that night I have to tell you a bit more about the road that led me to Bellini.

After Cairo I returned to Italy to sing a *Traviata* at La Fenice in 1956, with Alfredo Kraus as the young Germont. We became very good friends in Venice, exchanging Cairo stories (where Alfredo sang his first Duke in Verdi's *Rigoletto*) and talking about the music we loved.

Around this time I was having trouble with the *passaggio* to my head voice; it was not something that could be heard by the audience yet, but it worried me that I could feel the problem and it worried me more that my teacher did not know what to do about it. The problem was partly that I was singing too much and too many roles that were not good for me—at the time when my technique was simply not well formed. I had studied enough to provide good support and to breathe adequately, and I was singing successfully and often. But something now felt wrong in *Traviata*, my debut role. I had trouble with E-flat at the close of Act I, then I had trouble with the Bs and Cs. I was losing the top of my voice. I could hear it, particularly when I was singing with Alfredo Kraus: he had the technique for the high notes as part of his nature, the *passaggio* to head voice, the virtuosity that makes the voice both refined and natural in texture. I had been singing with my natural voice and dramatic temperament, but I could feel that if I did not do something soon the trouble would be apparent not just to me but to my audience.

Alfredo heard the problem as clearly as I did. He was frank. "You don't know how to sing correctly, Renata. You need a good teacher, and you should let me take you to mine. Mercedes Llopart is her name, and she will show you how to use your voice like an instrument." Now, this advice came not only from a good colleague but from the best *tenore di grazia* that I have ever heard, so I paid attention. From Barcelona to Milan he had had the same teacher, and she was in Milan now. So to Mercedes Llopart I went, and there was much to learn among her cozy pleiad in Milan. The great Catalan soprano had been

Toscanini's Marschallin at La Scala, and she would be my only teacher until the time of her death, when my husband took over.

When I showed Llopart what I had been doing, she immediately said, "No more *Butterfly*, no more *Pagliacci!* First you must learn to sing." I remember that she had on her piano a framed picture of a donkey showing his teeth, to caution singers to remember his whine and how to place the voice properly to avoid sounding like her smiling friend. She made me vocalize up to A, B-flat, and I could go no higher comfortably, I could not find the right position for the voice in the upper reaches. She helped me with my breathing and gave me exercises that I do to this day; and she developed my voice.

That first day she stopped me as I vocalized to a B-flat, she looked at the donkey's toothy, nasal whine frozen in the picture, and told me, "You will be fine, very fine. In three months of my technique you will be able to think high and smile. You will think of a flute's legato and sing that way. Don't think of breathing, that comes naturally when you sing right. You will sing coloratura." In three months I did have a great success with Donizetti's *L'elisir d'amore*, and soon I would be able to sing *La Sonnambula*.

Mercedes Llopart taught me the meaning of bel canto, all the time securing my support and steadying the tone; she hid the seams between registers and showed me how to reveal them when I chose to for good effect. That woman had so many vocal secrets to share. With her I prepared many roles in the Russian repertory which I had not considered before but which were very beautiful to sing, roles in *Khovanshchina*, *The Invisible City of Ktezh*, and especially *Pique Dame*, a Russian opera so French that it whetted my appetite for *Manon*.

Without Llopart I am sure that I would not have been able to enjoy a long career. It is dangerous to sing without a good technical foundation, and I was very fortunate to have been stopped and taught. Of course, even the maestri in those days were concerned for the vocal lives of their singers. Today so often they tend to find a beautiful natural voice, use it, and replace it with another when it wears out prematurely. It is very cruel. Great conductors like James Levine and Lorin Maazel, men who truly collaborate with singers, are hard to find; and even they do not have the time to show the concern for and to offer the guidance to young singers that Antonino Votto, Gianandrea Gavazzeni, and Tullio Serafin made a matter of habit.

I remember when I sang my first *Bohème* at La Scala. One month before the rehearsals began, Maestro Votto began to teach me the role of Mimi in his home, going over each phrase, each musical nuance. By the time I showed up onstage for the first rehearsal with the director, I knew Mimi intimately and we could really work on the drama. I was very fortunate.

At Llopart's insistence I began to study bel canto, although at the time that repertory did not interest me. I did prepare Norina in *Don Pasquale* and Adina in *L'elisir d'amore*, and I remember how Llopart made me pay so much attention to the words that the music came easily. Norina's entrance, for example, is a totally unprepared scene with cavatina and cabaletta, an operatic hurdle for which the soprano has no time to warm up musically or dramatically. *"Quel guardo il cavaliere . . . So anch'io la virtu magica."* It is a legato dream but it comes from a clever young woman who is more than just cute. It is this spark of intelligence that has to come through in the slow section if the audience is to get anything more than empty fireworks from the coloratura that follows; she caresses the violins against their grain at the opening of the aria, then she laughs and explains in deliciously wicked rhythms just how to use a glance on whom, how to win any man. The whole scene is a crescendo of emotion in a comic shade, and the audience should smile as much with this girl as about the situation.

With *Pique Dame*, which I first sang under Maestro Molinari-Pradelli, I began to understand that in opera acting and singing are inseparable. It was a good opera for me in 1955, because my studies with Llopart were going very well and I did not want to hurry her results too much. The role of Lisa is beautiful and lyric, dramatically melancholy in her cries of "I am yours" at the end of the first act, womanly and strong by the end; it also has very few high notes and all the music is ravishing.

I fell in love with Tchaikovsky, with his subtle musical portrayal of this girl in love who so often talks to herself in the same repeated note, a note of good sense. Tchaikovsky's Lisa is an oasis of sanity in the vast sands of desperation and compulsion. She is a beautiful creation, and I loved singing her. With Llopart I learned to pay as much attention to Lisa's words as to her music, and in the course of three or four years I sang *Pique Dame* in at least twenty Italian theaters, all the while improving my voice and regaining my top register.

I sang it in Italian, of course, not in Russian. Except at La Scala, opera was done in the language of the audience rather than in the original. It was not a bad compromise. I may be biased, but I think that Italian is good for music; it is a language that favors the voice. Come to think of it, my first *Faust* in French was at the Met in New York, because La Scala had us sing it in Italian. And it was fine, I think,

as were such exotic-sounding operas as *I pescatori di perle,
Damma di picche, Il franco cacciatore,* and many others.

I sang Bizet's Micaëla and Massenet's Sophie in Italian. I loved Micaëla; it is such a lovely, useful role for a
young singer: it allows one to act and to sing without
pushing the voice, and it has a beautiful enough aria that
the soprano who sings it can carry the evening without
having had to have the entire production on her shoulders.
Much as I loved her then, I confess that it is her rival who
interests me now, and I am studying more about Emma
Calvé and the soprano approach to Bizet's gypsy, hoping
to play Carmen myself. Massenet's Sophie I got to know
less well, singing it only twice and always with a longing
eye for her older sister Charlotte. I love Massenet, and it is
as Charlotte that I return to his opera *Werther* now. Unlike
Carmen, she is not really a mezzo-soprano role, I don't
think. She is not too dramatic; most of the role lies in the
middle voice. And she is very beautiful.

This was also a time for playing maids, like the
fabulous *Serva Padrona* of Pergolesi, and many others in
the lighter repertories. There were Weber's *Freischütz* and
Rossini's *Cambiale.* But then, between *Khovanshchina* in Turin and another *Traviata* in Venice, I remembered the
other score that I had taken with me to the convent from
Savona, Puccini's *Manon Lescaut.* I suggested to Llopart
that we work on it and I thought she would slap my hand.
"No," she said, "you cannot sing that, it's too dramatic.
Try the Massenet *Manon."* This time I disagreed with her,
but I said nothing because there were no offers for the
Puccini and there were possibilities for the Massenet; it
did fit my repertory at the time, and if my teacher thought
Puccini too strong perhaps I should follow her advice. For
now.

So I sang Massenet's Manon, but it was not my idea. I loved the role, of course, but one of the reasons that I eventually left Italy was that every role I sang seemed to have been somebody else's idea and not mine. The theaters had labeled me as a light singer; I knew that I was simply a soprano. The roles I sang in the 1950s did not hurt me, of course; I could keep the voice in good technical shape and not force the top. My tendency then as later was to give too much onstage, so following a lighter repertory for about ten years was healthy; but somebody else always chose, and I was beginning not to like that. "Sing this, don't sing that, stay away from Puccini" were all too familiar, and I was too young and too worried to make my own decisions.

I learned much from Mercedes Llopart, and later from Lorenzo Anselmi and others; I would like to teach some of what I have learned, and I remember that my first pupil was Dick Cavett: I gave my first master class on his talk show a few years ago. I told him that he was not quite ready for the stage, but I enjoyed myself very much. Since then I have begun to give classes occasionally. But I am getting ahead of my own story.

At twenty-three I was singing in every major theater in Italy, and I was afraid to make a mistake, to enter the dramatic repertory too soon. Before *La Sonnambula* I sang almost everything except Bellini; my *Butterfly* and *Pagliacci* had been in smaller theaters and my important career was still ahead. When Maestro Tonini agreed with Llopart and said, "Don't even think about *Manon Lescaut*, try the Massenet *Manon*; now there's a role for you," I went to a French coach in Milan and began studying the role for Covent Garden.

Manon is a close cousin to the roles I would sing after

Amina, heroines like Lucia and Gilda, Norina, Adina, and of course always Violetta. With a special language coach I worked on acting in French, trying to remember all I could from having lived so near the French Riviera as I was growing up. The debut made me very happy, and it was not until almost twenty years later that I arrived at my first choice, Puccini's *Manon Lescaut*. The two operas are of course different sides of the same woman, and I prefer to discuss both together. But *Manon Lescaut* happened for me only after my success in *Butterfly*, when I realized that if one can sing that one can sing any Puccini, even *Turandot*. If I was chosen to sing the Massenet, I am the one who chose the Puccini. But the road was long, and one of its signposts was the music of Bellini, with the spirit of his romantic age and the memory of its greatest singer, Maria Malibran.

Three

Sleepwalking with Malibran

Some time ago the composer Gian Carlo Menotti told me
a story about the time when he and Samuel Barber were
living by a lake near Vienna. He had a neighbor, a baroness, who would ask them to dinner but had a habit of
excusing herself after eating to go to chapel and pray. The
young composer was curious and asked if he might join
her in prayer one time, although he was not a religious
man. He was fascinated to find that the chapel was a room
with a table and that the prayer sessions were séances at
which this lady would try to communicate with her
daughter, who had died very young. The baroness went
into a trance, calling out, "Doodly, Doodly," her daughter's name. Gian Carlo did not laugh; he was very moved.
And he admitted that, although he saw nothing, perhaps
the reason was that he did not believe; and perhaps this
woman who so completely believed did in fact see. Religion and magic are myterious sisters. At any rate, here
Gian Carlo began to realize that skepticism is a destructive
force and belief its opposite. He began to think of what
would become his opera *The Medium*, and he kept the name
Doodly for one of the spirits the protagonist calls.

In 1956 some friends mentioned backstage that they
were going to a séance and asked me to go along. I had
never heard of such things, certainly not in all my years at
the Canossian convent. But I was curious, so I went. I
went for the experience, but I wasn't expecting much
more than entertainment, and I was not the one who
wanted to ask anything of any spirits; there were others in
the group who wanted just that.

In the darkened room with an old mahogany table at

the center and little else around, this very respectable lady offered us coffee and talked for a bit after introductions; then she asked us to be very still and for a long time we held hands while nothing was said. Then she began to speak, first in an unintelligible whisper, later in a disembodied voice, very musical and distant. She talked to me, saying that I must sing what she sang; she repeated it. She seemed very sad and talked of dying young, of having wanted to go on singing forever. Then she said that I would sing for her, that I must sing her roles. At that point the medium began to make writing motions on the table, fast and then faster. Someone put a pen in her hand and she began scribbling fast on white paper, one sheet, then another, then ten more; finally a name could be made out: Maria Malibran.

Years later the director Giorgio de Lullo made me a present of a letter from Maria Malibran in which in 1834 the great singer talked about her fears for the reception of Donizetti's *Maria Stuarda* at La Scala; the letter hangs in my study in Gonzaga today. I had kept the sheets from that séance in Milan, and the signatures are identical. In 1956, however, I had not heard much about Malibran, and I did not take the séance very seriously until some months later when I had to.

Maria Malibran was born in 1808 as Maria Felicità García, the daughter of Manuel García, who was possibly the greatest singing teacher in history. She was probably a contralto, but her voice extended well into the soprano stratosphere and she became one of the most revered singers of the romantic era. If we can believe the reports of the day, her voice was not conventionally beautiful and was replete with trouble spots and audible register breaks. She was also extremely temperamental when it came to her music, and one time she punched a tenor in London during a performance of *La Sonnambula* because he was not showing any emotion onstage. This outburst notwithstanding, she was Bellini's favorite Amina, although the role was written for and premiered with a more conventionally lovely diva, Giuditta Pasta. After hearing La Malibran in his opera, he wrote to his friend Florimo that he had become hoarse from shouting "Brava!" and that he felt as if he were in heaven. Soon he did go to heaven, at the age of thirty-three. And his diva followed: she was thrown from a horse while pregnant with her first child. She lost the child and, a few days later, her life. In her prime. She never sang Bellini again.

La Sonnambula, one of Malibran's greatest roles, is a jewel of bel canto. It takes place during the early days of the nineteenth century in a lovely Swiss village where the townspeople are gathered to celebrate the betrothal of Amina to Elvino with shouts of *"Viva, viva Amina."* Everyone seems to think that this is a perfect match except for the discontented innkeeper, Lisa, who is herself in love with Elvino. Amina greets her friends in the beautiful *"Care compagne, e voi teneri amici"* and shows her love for her fiancé and for her family. The appearance of a handsome stranger makes Elvino a little jealous, but the innocent Amina cries at the suggestion that she could ever be unfaithful, and her tears bring love back to Elvino's eyes.

At the inn it is Lisa who flirts with the stranger, but he remains alone in his room. Later that evening he is shocked to find a young woman—not Lisa, but Amina—walking in her sleep and calling to Elvino. The embarrassed man leaves through the window, but Lisa has been watching the room with ideas of her own and now she uses the situation to compromise the innocent girl. She calls Elvino, she calls the whole village in fact; and as Act I closes Amina is left alone, wondering if anyone will believe her innocence as she wakes in a strange man's bed.

The villagers eventually ask the stranger himself what happened, but in the meantime Elvino has taken up with the evil Lisa and the two are about to be married. It takes yet another sleepwalk to make Elvino believe Amina. She appears walking on the roof and then on a narrow board, at risk of falling and killing herself. She dreams that Elvino is at the altar with another girl, at which point there is a delicate echo in the orchestra of the happiness of which Amina sang earlier. All the musical parts are of one cloth, woven into the most perfect pages of bel canto in *"Ah! non credea mirarti,"* where Amina laments the fate of the fading flower that Elvino had given her. She awakes and is believed to be innocent. Then, reunited with her love, she sings the thrilling *"Ah! non giunge uman pensiero";* human thoughts cannot quite encompass all the joy Amina feels. In her love she is reassured and with love she will rise to the heavens.

I did not know this perfect opera when I went to that séance in Milan and had no plans to study it and no prospects for singing it in the future. The closest I had come to it was La Scala's offer of the role of Lisa, which I had turned down after my debut in *La Wally*. Other things occupied my mind. I was making my London debut in 1957, in a season of Italian opera produced by S. A. Gorlinsky at the Stoll Theater, where I sang Violetta opposite Kraus's Alfredo, followed by Adina, Mimi, and Donna Elvira. I was in love with Mozart during my appearances in *Don Giovanni* and I wondered if I should prepare Fiordiligi or the Countess. Eventually my love affair with Mozart would become recital flirtations, since when it came to learning new roles there always seemed to be a Verdi or Puccini role that interested me more.

But with Mozart, Puccini, Donizetti, and Verdi in the works, I had no trouble saying no to La Scala when they offered me Lisa once more.

In the meantime I was offered my first two recording contracts: a recital on EMI for which Walter Legge engaged me after auditioning me for the role of the Italian singer in *Capriccio* by Richard Strauss (I did not sing that role, but I was interested in making my first recital album). And my first operatic recording, the role of Glauce in Cherubini's *Medea*, with Maria Callas in the title role: the sessions for this Ricordi recording were to begin in early September 1957.

Now I needed money. The London season had left me not very rich and travel expenses had taken care of my savings. When La Scala called about Lisa I had turned them down because I did not need the money that desperately, but when they called back and asked me to go as a cover on a tour to the Edinburgh Festival, I said yes before even knowing which roles I would be covering for, as long as they were protagonists. I did not want to work onstage at La Scala in a secondary role, but I could use a job, and covering was a real job with pay. It would not be a bad career move since I would surely be out of sight; everyone knew that singers just do not cancel such prestigious engagements. I was sure that I would not sing, that I would travel and have time to study while in Edinburgh. When the management asked me if I had any preference as to whom to cover I saw a greater chance for studying and learning and replied immediately.

"Yes, Maria Callas. I want to cover Callas."

She was the most exciting singer I had ever seen in

my years of Sundays at La Scala from the convent, and I was sure to learn something from the trip.

Then I was asked if I knew *La Sonnambula* and I lied, of course, and said that I had learned it earlier. I was told, by the prompter Naldini, I remember, to come to a rehearsal with Maestro Votto the next day because Callas was not available and the maestro needed an orchestral run-through. Now I was worried. I knew Antonino Votto, one of the great conductors; I did not know the role, and I was to rehearse it the next day. I ran out to get the score and stayed up all night.

The next day I went to La Scala to rehearse, looking very sleepy but still not knowing the music. The rehearsal began with the concertato passage from Act II, which I could sight-read. Then came a break after which the final scene was to be sung. Now Votto had been like a father to me. He had been at my first *Traviata* and he had always had only encouraging words for me. He trusted me.

"Scottina," he said, "you are here. Brava." Then he asked me if I knew the score.

"I studied it last year, Maestro. But I don't remember it very well. Would it be all right if I took the score onstage with me for the words?"

"Don't worry, Scottina, Naldini is here. He will prompt you," and he looked at me with a suspicious smile.

"The truth is, Maestro, I have to look at the music."

"All right, Scottina, don't worry. Take the score."

So I went on for the first rehearsal of "*Ah! non credea* . . ." and "*Ah! non giunge,*" score in hand, with an assistant director motioning me here and there as I sang and Maestro Votto reassuring me from the pit. The only way I was able to do it was because I was so young and so rash. When you start out people tend to treat you with a lot of sympathy and encouragement, and La Scala is a very good theater. The chorus mothered me and everyone helped, from the prompter and the conductor to even the tenors in the chorus. When you are a big star, going to rehearsal unprepared only brings out feelings like "Ha, let's see how she can manage." This reaction is as strong an incentive always to be prepared as the responsibility to the public and the music. But in the beginning everybody is so sweet. So I sang my first rehearsal, and afterward I signed my contract. Two days later we left.

On the train to Edinburgh I shared a cabin with a very nice *comprimaria* who kept telling me not to worry. I laughed and said that I wasn't worried. "When you cover Callas you don't sing. She will never cancel this tour, and if she did La Scala would probably cancel the performance."

I made friends in Edinburgh, and I ran into people and critics who had seen me in the London *Elisir* or *Don Giovanni* a few months earlier. We went to the theater but I didn't get a ticket for *Sonnambula:* it was a very small theater, completely sold out, and the singers were not given seats at all. So I stood in the wings as Callas began *"Care compagne . . . ,"* saw that she was in fine voice, and left for the hotel to study for the upcoming *Medea.*

Maestro Serafin himself had asked for me to be in the recording, and the producer, Nanni Ricordi, had been very pleased with the audition. The sessions were to begin the day after the tour, so I spent my time in Edinburgh studying the role of Glauce. I had seen *Medea* only once, with Callas and Bernstein; but I was too young to really appreciate it, and I surely did not remember much of the role of Medea's most innocent victim.

The next night I again did not have seats for the opera, Donizetti's *L'elisir d'amore,* so I was in my room with Glauce when I got a call at six-thirty from Votto. Rosanna Carteri, the Adina of the evening, had canceled. It seems that there was no cover because the soprano who was supposed to do that job had to sing *Il Matrimonio Segreto* the following evening and she refused to sing both.

The review of the first night's *Elisir* had been less than generous, and one of the critics wondered in print why La Scala had not brought in this tour that nice Renata Scotto who had sung such a beautiful Adina in London last May. So somebody in the company noticed that I was in my hotel room doing nothing, and I was asked if I could be ready in half an hour. I said yes. I was twenty-three and I well knew that the best policy was always to be ready and never to be afraid. I looked through the score as the dresser labored around me: Rosanna was tall and slim, I was short and not slim; some adjustments had to be made in the costumes. In minutes I was onstage with Giuseppe di Stefano and Sesto Bruscantini. The curtain went up on time and came down to very loud and long applause.

The day after *Elisir* I learned that there was also no Callas for the last performance of *La Sonnambula.*

The production of *Sonnambula* had been so successful that La Scala decided to add an extra performance at what was supposed to be the end of the run. Callas had not been consulted before the announcement, however, and she did not have a contract for this extra performance. She had other plans—a party at Elsa Maxwell's—and she had no intention of singing the extra Amina. La Scala expected that she would change her mind, but in fact she had left Edinburgh. Votto knew this the night of *Elisir,* but he had thought it best to tell me only afterward. I never met Callas during this tour.

Many artists have their big chance by replacing other artists; it is a fantastic tale that happens often. Callas herself replaced Margherita Carosio in a Venice *Puritani*, in which she had one of her early successes. Even Beverly Sills made her belated and spectacular debut at La Scala replacing me when I was having my first child; and the same thing happened to the young Katia Ricciarelli, who was launched on her international career thanks to my second child. This *Sonnambula* was my chance, and if *Elisir* had been a good risk, this was an even bigger but more important one.

I had two days to prepare, and I spent every one of those hours with Votto at the piano. The vocal exercise was quite good for the coloratura, actually; but even I was surprised at how fast I was working and how much energy I was summoning. Votto was so proud, so reassuring; he knew that if I succeeded that success would be his as well. On her departure Callas had told reporters, "I am leaving the role to a younger colleague who will cover herself with glory," but the reporters started rumors of a fight with Callas, and La Scala organized a press conference for me the day before the performance. It was my first press conference ever.

"Are you afraid of what Maria Callas may do to you, Signorina Scotto?"

"I beg your pardon?" The gentlemen of the press were showing definitely yellow hues on this occasion.

"Is it true that Callas threatened you?"

"No, of course not. I have not met Maria Callas, actually. But I admire her immensely. She is a great singer."

The questions were all so ridiculous. It was many years before I believed that people could be that blind and bitchy about a great singer, and when I did the moment was not a happy one. For now, I just wondered why they all assumed that Callas had done anything to me. No, she did not hit me. No, I repeated, I really had not met her. Yes, I did admire her very much. And so on.

By the final rehearsal with Votto I knew the role well enough to go onstage. It would take me a good ten years to understand Amina, and I have spent much of my career loving and learning this role. But even after three days of work some things were clear and some changes had to be made in the production. Originally in Luchino Visconti's production, Amina had been decked out with jewels and made to look like the romantic dancer Maria Taglioni; her movements were stylized and balletic and she seemed to belong not to a Swiss village but to the world of dance. It worked beautifully for Callas, but I could not help thinking that Amina was a poor country girl, alone and bewildered, very young—all things I knew about.

So I took off the white gloves and the jewelry and began to identify with the character by remembering my own life: I had no boyfriend, and I was so alone in those days away from my family; I had not always had a lot to eat, and I was certainly not rich now; I had known a village like Amina's where everyone knew me and my nostalgia for Savona made its way into Amina's opening aria to the villagers. Later I would study more about Bellini and his period, later I would portray Amina even more realistically and romantically than in that night in Edinburgh. But for now I felt that the story was simple, simply Italian, and very moving. The coloratura was not for show, and the costuming and stage movements should mirror the very real, very sweet dilemma of this innocent young peasant.

That night before the performance I had a dream, a

beautiful revelation in my sleep. The image of Maria Malibran appeared, as vividly as she had to the medium in Milan months earlier. She smiled and reassured me. She told me to take my entrance calmly and think of the public as my love. She told me to trust the music completely because from my mouth would come her voice. I woke up so happy. It was only a dream, yes. But I felt so good, so ready to sing. The encouragement has never been quite so direct as it was on this occasion, but I have felt it and still feel it today. I never begin to work on a new interpretation, especially of a Bellini or Donizetti heroine, without having Malibran not far from my heart.

On September 3, 1957, my first *Sonnambula* changed my life. It took courage to replace a great diva, and my success was noted. I became a celebrity, I could choose my roles, I felt more responsible, and I began to grow as an artist. That night was very beautiful. I was in very good voice; the nerves helped and my dream helped even more. All of Italian opera can be heard in *"Ah! non credea,"* and I truly felt it inside me for the first time that night in Edinburgh. The applause at the end would not stop, with ten, twelve solo calls until Maestro Votto had to come out holding my hand and make a speech to the audience.

"You are fantastic," he said in his best English, "but you have to let her go. She has to take a train to London soon, to go back to Milan tomorrow for the first session of her first record. So let her go."

It *was* fantastic. Fans followed me to the train station and photographers followed me and the fans. I was still in a daze when I arrived at the *Medea* recording session the next day. I was greeted by Tullio Serafin and Nanni Ricordi, and then I met my colleagues Miriam Pirazzini, Mirto Picchi, and Giuseppe Modesti.

In a short while Callas arrived and we were finally introduced. She said to me, "I heard that you did very well last night. *Brava, molto brava. Bene.*" And I thanked her. I was very pleased by her compliment, for I had truly admired her since the first time I saw her in *Norma* and *Gioconda* in my student days. Callas was the first in our time to realize the importance of the words in bel canto, the one who treated the voice as a human faculty and not as a coloratura machine; she taught us that coloratura is a servant of the music and that the text as well as the music must be communicated to the audience. Yes, it had been a beautiful week and now I was very pleased.

Then we got to work and Serafin, who was never shy about making cuts in a score, suggested to Callas that perhaps her first aria would be more effective in a shorter form, without some of the repetitions. Callas paused for a second and then fixed her eyes on Serafin and her hands toward me, and she said "No. No, Maestro, no. If you want to cut anything, cut Glauce's aria."

I was stunned. Glauce's aria is all that Glauce has to sing; without it in the recording, any chorister could have sung the role. It was not a very courteous thing to do, but as Serafin refused to cut my aria I did not think very much about it until years later when repeating the story seemed to violate some mythical taboo. But that is a tale of another time.

After *La Sonnambula* I returned to La Scala in 1958 for a new production of *L'elisir d'amore* with Di Stefano and Bastianini, my colleagues in the hurried Edinburgh *Elisir;* and in a new *Hansel and Gretel,* my first, with Fiorenza Cossotto playing my older brother. In 1959 there was a new *Don Pasquale* in Turin with Serafin, followed by a new *Bohème* with Gianni Raimondi (replacing Di Stefano on short notice), Bastianini, and Boris Christoff. I made many recordings in these two years, and perhaps my favorite was *Rigoletto* under Maestro Gianandrea Gavazzeni with the great Ettore Bastianini as my father and my old friend Alfredo Kraus as my love.

Real love came soon as well. Dickens might have made it more complicated, but I cannot imagine how. In the spring of 1956 a young violin virtuoso joined the orchestra at La Scala; he was soon to become its first violinist. I was in London at the time singing Donna Elvira. When I returned and began to work in preparation for the Edinburgh trip, I scarcely noticed that the company was not traveling with the full orchestra and that any musicians who did not wish to go on the tour were easily excused. The violinist did not go, and he remained in Milan as I sang my *Sonnambula*. But who should be there at my first recording session but him? And why am I going on about a violinist from La Scala? Because his name is Lorenzo Anselmi, and he would soon become the most important man in my life.

Four

Lucia and the Wedding Feast

(Preceding page, photo: Luigi E. Serra) Left, after the war we were able to return to Savona and I had my first communion. Mother made the dress. Top left, still in Savona with my sister Luciana. Top right, a recital with the great Beniamino Gigli in 1954, shortly after my debut. We sang the Cherry Duet from Mascagni's *L'amico Fritz*. (photo: Cinefoto Pandolfi, Pesaro) Bottom, in Cairo, with my mother and a tenor. It was my first trip outside Italy, and I sang Menotti's *Amelia al ballo*. I returned in 1955.

Opposite page, top left, my marriage to Lorenzo Anselmi in Savona. (photo: Dufoto, Rome) Top right, in Moscow during La Scala's visit to the Bolshoi. (photo: Piccagliani, La Scala) Bottom, my most important role, that of mother. Here is my daughter, Laura, at left and my son, Filippo, at right.

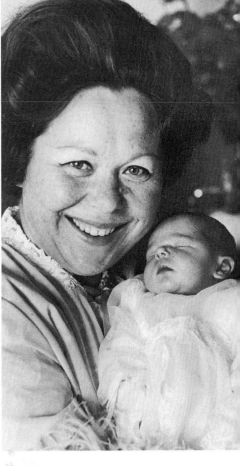

I QUATTRO GRANDI DEL MET

New York. Quattro "grandi" della lirica italiana si sono incontrati dietro le quinte del nuovo Metropolitan di New York in occasio di un'applauditissima "Bohème". Ecco, da sinistra: Renata Scotto; Franco Corelli; Renata Tebaldi e Licia Albanese. Franco Core e Renata Tebaldi indossano ancora gli abiti con cui hanno interpretato l'opera pucciniana. Alcuni giorni prima, sulle stesse sce la Scotto aveva festeggiato la sua 100ᵃ interpretazione della "Traviata". La stampa americana ha dato gran rilievo all'avvenimen

Top, after celebrating my hundredth *Traviata* while performing the role in New York, the press back home added my name to those of the "Grandi Italiani" of the Met. (photo: *Gente*, April 19, 1967) Bottom, with Ann Miller and Mickey Rooney.

Opposite page, in opera I am always someone else, but in recitals I am free to be exposed, to be myself. I can be Renata Scotto, singer. (photo: Jorge Fama, Buenos Aires)

Top, golf is not my sport. (photo: Henry Grossman) Bottom, I did a little better as the Met's very own shortstop in a game against the Emory University coaches. (photo: Mary Cheatham)

Opposite page, top left, my parents' golden wedding anniversary. Top right, at home with my mother and daughter. Bottom, signing autographs.

Lorenzo Anselmi was born in Pomponesco, in the province of Mantua, in 1933, and at the age of four his family moved to nearby Gonzaga, the old summer home of Isabella d'Este; it is such a tiny hidden treasure that most maps do not show it. From an old Emilian family, Lorenzo's father was a violinist and his mother a teacher—a school principal, in fact, by the time Lorenzo entered school. At the age of five his father gave him his first violin, and I remember his telling me that he would compose little songs on the violin until his eighth birthday, when he began musical lessons in earnest with his father. His younger sister played the piano, and the family delighted in their duets. Lorenzo's sister was not interested for long and soon stopped playing, but he could talk of little else and when he turned twelve, as the war ended, he was sent to the Parma Conservatory to become a real musician. He would commute from Gonzaga to Parma four times a week, hurrying to his classes with the very strict and renowned Ermanno Marchesi.

The war years had not been easy in this part of the country either, and the family did not soon forget the horrible stories of the concentration camp for political prisoners that was only two blocks away or the sounds of partisan bombs that once came close enough to damage their home. The end of the war found these Mantuans, along with most Italians, happy to be at peace and struggling to find happiness again. For Lorenzo music was everything. He began playing professionally when he was very young, even before finishing at the conservatory. In his last year there he entered the Corelli Competition for young violinists, for which each conservatory chose a candidate in preliminary rounds to send to Rome and compete for a place with the famous Corelli Ensemble and a concert tour. The Parma Conservatory faculty decided not to have preliminary competitions but rather to select Lorenzo unanimously, so in 1955 he went off to Rome. And he won. He had just turned twenty-two and was faced with the prospect of the army as well as that of graduation. But a mild pneumonia kept him out of uniform when he was called, and his teacher advised him not to pass up the tour and to receive his diploma later.

For the next six months he went on a tour of eighty-two concerts in Canada and the United States followed by appearances in San Juan and Havana. In the Cuban capital the Corelli musicians were forced to remain in the Hotel Nacional instead of performing in the Pro Arte Auditorium because there was revolutionary unrest in the streets between the hotel and the theater.

When Lorenzo returned to Parma he accelerated his studies with private lessons and convinced the faculty to give him his exams early, so he received his diploma only months after his return from his first professional tour. He was asked to return to the United States for another tour that would have included some solo appearances, but this time the financial details were not very promising— Lorenzo has always had the best head for business in the family—and he said no. He decided he wanted no more of touring with chamber groups or of running around to recitals, so when there were open auditions for the orchestra at La Scala, he tried out and was accepted. He had never seen an opera and wasn't very interested in vocal music except for one voice he had heard on the radio while he was studying that had forced him to listen. It was the voice of Callas. Later he told me that the only other voice that affected him this way was mine, and in fact that has much to do with how we met. But we only spoke for a few moments during those *Medea* sessions. I did not have much to do on the record, and I was still very shy with boys, so I left.

During the season we were both at La Scala, of course —he always and I often enough. He remembers hearing during *Bohème* and *Elisir* a voice that forced his attention, that he had to listen to. He found out who it was and remembered that it was the same girl from the *Medea* record. So he managed to get my phone number and called me. He introduced himself as the first violinist from the orchestra, then he said how much my singing had touched him, and I believed him and liked him instantly. "I just wanted to tell you that," he said and hung up. I was intrigued. Ten minutes later he called again, saying that he looked forward to seeing me in the theater. There we did meet, and this time the conversation was a little longer; he asked me if perhaps we might get together after work. He was tall and dark, and he had the deepest Latin eyes I had ever seen.

I remember that I drove on our first date—not the Cadillac that Del Monaco had predicted but a beat-up Fiat made in Turin. We went to play miniature golf after a morning rehearsal. We had played two or three holes when a thunderstorm forced us to a cafe where we talked for hours. After that I could seldom stand to be away from him for very long, and the relationship grew very naturally and sweetly. He gave me the wisest advice on my singing that I had heard. In those days I was compared to so many sopranos; I was complimented as the new Toti Dal Monte, the new Lina Pagliughi, the new Mafalda

Favero, or the new anybody else. With Lorenzo I felt much better about wanting to be just the new Renata Scotto. He saw that while I sang the lyric repertory my voice was not *leggiera* only, he made me see that it was sensuous. And if *Sonnambula* opened up many new doors, after a new production at La Scala of Glinka's *A Life for the Tsar* I could have whatever I wanted, so big was the success and the satisfaction I derived from that opera. But I am getting ahead of myself.

In 1958 Nanni Ricordi asked if I would be interested in recording Donizetti's *Lucia di Lammermoor,* with Di Stefano and Bastianini and the Scala Orchestra and Chorus. I had never sung the role, but I did not want to pass up the chance to work with Di Stefano, and as I was to be given time to prepare the role I accepted. I sang it in the manner of the tradition I had received, with cuts within the score but adding many new notes of my own. I sang the duet with the flute with much ornamentation, and I added the E-flat.

The recording schedule was a little strange, because Di Stefano slept during the day and would only record after 10 P.M.; my hours, not long after my convent days, were quite the opposite of that. I was very sleepy for most of the duets. But after recording the wedding feast and the sextet late on two weekend nights, I had the studio to myself at a normal hour to record the Mad Scene. Now this was not a role that I had sung onstage, and though later I would come to know Lucia very well and truly enter her musical mind, the cadenza from the first part of the Mad Scene will always take me out of character and turn me into myself again. There is a very good reason for this. I sang alone and then with the flute, then alone again, while Maestro Nino Sanzogno looked on. I noticed that

Lorenzo's eyes were fixed on my lips as I sang, that he followed each word I uttered as if he were breathing my breath, feeling my song. He understood so well what I was doing, and I could not take my eyes off him—I don't think I looked at the conductor once in that scene. Lorenzo and I had never talked of love before this day, we had just been the very best of friends. But after that recording session for the Cetra *Lucia* I understood that I loved him. And he understood too. He walked me home after the recording session. And he asked me to marry him.

The news was greeted with much joy by all our friends; everyone knew that it was a perfect match almost before we ourselves had realized it. We had many things to work out, many plans to make. My career took me all over Europe, and his was fixed in Milan. It was not easy. Eventually Lorenzo decided to leave La Scala and dedicate his musicianship and his love to help me, and he became not only the best husband but also the finest teacher and manager that any singer could hope for. He would always be what I knew he was the first time we were caught in the rain: my truest friend.

On June 2, 1960, we were married in the Church of San Giuseppe in Albissola Mare, just outside of Savona. I think that everyone who had been at my first *Traviata* managed to come to the church. My mother supervised my wedding dress and the long, beautiful veil, made in one of the best boutiques in Milan's Montenapoleone. The rehearsal pianist from La Scala, Franco Verganti, played the Wedding March from *Lohengrin* on the organ, and the tenor Nicola Monti sang César Franck's *Panis Angelicus* after Lorenzo and I took our vows. We left the church and took the traditional wedding walk through a huge crowd of smiling friends and then we left for our honeymoon on the Riviera, San Remo, Monte Carlo, and Cannes.

At the end of June we returned for a solo concert at La Scala where I sang Rossini's *Soirées Musicales,* then Gilda in Rome on the heels of the recording, followed by a trip to Chicago, my first and Lorenzo's second, for Mimi and Micaëla.

It was hectic and a lot of fun in those days, all a bit confusing. The dizzying honeymoon mentality lasted well into the working season. I remember how on tour with the Royal Opera, Covent Garden, one late afternoon that year we were looking around for something to do in the evening. "How about a movie?" So we checked the newspaper but there were no Italian or French movies in town and I didn't feel like struggling in English on my day off (my English has improved since those days). "What about the opera? Now there's a good idea." And it was a good idea; we could not find the information in the paper; there was the wrong listing for that evening. So we called the theater.

"Excuse me, what opera do you have tonight?"

"*La Bohème,* at seven o'clock." It was six.

"No, you must be mistaken; tonight is not *Bohème. Bohème* is Thursday. I know, I am in it."

"Lady, if you are in *La Bohème* you'd better hurry." He was right. And Mimi made an unusually breathless entrance that evening. And I loved it and her, and I loved Micaëla; and there was always Violetta, often and better for me every time. And *Lucia di Lammermoor,* the opera that had brought us together, would soon mark a treasured moment onstage but also a break with La Scala. With Lorenzo I could live through it all. I was not alone anymore.

Five

From Milan to Moscow
with La Scala

Glinka's *A Life for the Tsar* is the most Russian opera that I
have sung, and the role of Antonida is one of the most
beautiful. From the opening, as Antonida tries to calm the
fears of her father, Ivan Susanin, to the end in Moscow's
Red Square, where a glorious trio highlights the crowning
of the new monarch, it is an opera of strong and effective
echoes. The production was a great triumph, and it was
followed by an even greater one with *Rigoletto* at La Scala.

If earlier in my career I had said yes too soon or erro-
neously, those days were ending with Lorenzo's encouragement. I only took what I knew would be good for me,
and I hoped only to grow better each time. I studied *Rigoletto* with Lorenzo before this new production, noticing
afresh the meaning of the words and assuring myself of
the dramatic necessity of even the most florid passages of
Gilda's music. My father was to be Bastianini, with whom
I had made my first *Rigoletto* recording, and as I rehearsed
the duets I became this hunchback's unfortunate daughter
for the first time. I found the innocence in the voice that is
the key to making *"Caro nome"* a naive and disarming con-
fession of first love and not a fiendish vocal exercise; and I
began to understand the transformation of this abused girl
into womanhood as her final sacrifice approaches in the
last act.

The evening was difficult. Bastianini was not in his
best voice on opening night and the Scala claque started to
boo and shout bets that he would not finish. Audiences
that have been so loving can turn so cruel in one night
that the thought is truly horrifying. Gianni Raimondi was
nervous from all the commotion and his voice thinned out

to the point that he was being booed as well. I did not want to be caught in this particular *corrida*, I just wanted to sing Verdi and try to save the evening. I think I did, and La Scala was very grateful. I was asked what role I would like to do next and when I said, immediately, Violetta, the director Ghiringhelli agreed that it was a very good idea.

At this point I had been doing both *La Traviata* and *Lucia di Lammermoor* all over Italy, and those were the two operas that I would have liked to bring to Milan if La Scala wanted to mount new productions. I remember a *Traviata* in Naples with Gavazzeni when, after the phrase *"Amami, Alfredo"* and Violetta's exit, the public simply would not stop applauding until I came out again, and then they refused to quiet down and instead demanded an encore; this went on for ten minutes, and Maestro Gavazzeni had to turn around and make a speech to the audience about the impossibility of repeating anything, much less a phrase. Just like that, in the middle of an act!

When I was recording *La Traviata* in 1961, during the sessions we heard rumors that La Scala was going to mount a new production of the opera. Lorenzo and I spoke with Ghiringhelli and he agreed that it was a wonderful idea and that the record and the production could create nice publicity together. But he said that the *Traviata* was not for the following season and that if I could wait he would like me to sing *Madama Butterfly;* I agreed, of course, and signed the contract for *Butterfly*. But I did not forget *Traviata* because I really never could. I had never left the opera since my first one at the Teatro Nuovo. I knew Violetta completely; it was my best role and the one that the public wanted to see. It was a role that I wanted to bring to La Scala, and I was willing to wait. But no sooner had I signed the contract for *Butterfly* than I heard from my friend Mirella Freni that she was doing a new *Traviata* that same season, directed by Franco Zeffirelli and conducted by Herbert von Karajan. I could not believe it.

We confronted Ghiringhelli and he confessed that he had made the agreement with the director and conductor before he talked with me, and that Zeffirelli had said that I did not *look* right for the part of Violetta. So the head of La Scala went along without questioning that judgment and without regard to his agreement with me. At the same time the announcement was made that La Scala would be participating in a historic first visit to the Bolshoi Theater in Moscow; the repertory would include *Turandot, Il Trovatore, La Bohème,* and *Lucia di Lammermoor.* The Lucia was to be the Australian soprano Joan Sutherland.

Before I heard of the Bolshoi plans I had sworn never to go back to La Scala as long as Ghiringhelli was there. A new production of *La Traviata* in Geneva coincided within a few days with La Scala's. The Milanese reviews of mine were fabulous, but the reviews for Von Karajan and Zeffirelli were poor despite Freni's beautiful Violetta. There was some talk in the press of a rivalry and fights between me and Freni, and later in the season between me and Anna Moffo, who alternated with Freni as Violetta. There was no truth to this; I love Mirella. Then the editorials joined the music reviews in writing about the Bolshoi visit. My recent *Lucia* in Turin had been a critical triumph, and the more patriotic writers began a campaign in the press, saying that it was a disgrace of Italy's greatest theater to visit Russia for the first time and not to take an Italian Lucia, especially when they could have me.

La Scala's visit depended on government funds, and apparently there were many letters not only to the newspapers but to various ministries demanding that they take my *Lucia* to Moscow. La Scala reconsidered, or actually just simply considered, since I had told them goodbye the season before the visit to Russia and we had not discussed *Lucia* at all. I accepted. In doing so I gave a press interview in *L'Europeo* at which I stressed that I was going to Russia with La Scala for my country and for the company as well, since my fight was with Ghiringhelli and not with La Scala. I saw the visit as an important musical ambassadorship to a new country for all of us. And I said that when Ghiringhelli left, if La Scala needed me, I would return.

In Moscow the Scala publicity machinery ignored the fact that I was there, and for some reason they gave the great mezzo-soprano Giulietta Simionato the same treatment. I waited until my *Lucia* to see if things would change, but they did not. Still, the Moscow *Lucia* became one of my happiest memories, all because of the public.

The production was handsome, and the audience was filled with murmurs of admiration as the curtain went up on the second scene, at a fountain near the grave of Lucia's mother. Lucia has ignored her brother's warnings and has come to meet her lover Edgardo. She tells Alisa of a ghost she has seen near the fountain, a mysterious spirit that seems to tell of a tragic end for herself and Edgardo. Here, in the aria *"Regnava nel silenzio,"* the mood is established that Lucia's madness is to be more surrealistic than psychotic, more romantic; in other words, the opera is not Freud but bel canto, and it must be done in the right style. At the Bolshoi we managed to move from Lucia's declamations of unrestrained love in *"Quando rapito in estasi"* through Edgardo's entrance and the love promises of the last duet all in one thrust to avoid applause and not break the mood.

In the second act, as Lucia's brother tricks her into accepting a marriage of convenience to Arturo for the sake of the family, Lucia must move from defiance of her brother and unquestioned love for Edgardo through doubts as she is shown the forged letter to total loss of hope in the duet *"Soffriva nel pianto."* Her downfall has begun, and vocally that duet is of a piece with the sumptuous wedding feast at Lammermoor Castle. There is one of Donizetti's most joyous choruses. *"Per te d'immenso giubilo"* is a cruel foil for the sadness of Lucia's life, as she loses her love irrevocably and eventually loses her mind. When the Mad Scene does come, it is a wholly musical portrayal; everything is in the score.

On a few occasions directors have suggested to me that Lucia should have blood all over her gown in this scene, to indicate that she has just murdered her new husband on their wedding night. I say, nonsense. The blood is in the music. *Lucia* is not verismo, but it also needs no such vulgar help in the costumes. Only when she is sung as a string of coloratura arias might it be a nice idea to make her costume bloody: it would be one way to let the audience know what has happened. I prefer to sing it. And I had never sung it as well as at the Bolshoi that night.

The ovation was incredible in the cadenza, that same cadenza that had brought Lorenzo and me together. He was standing offstage and could not believe it either. It was truly unlike anything I had ever experienced: the applause continued and continued in sounds not at all like the Met's or La Scala's. The Russians clapped until they all joined in a definite pulse which then became faster and faster until beat clashed with beat in an explosion of applause; then they began all over. It is amazing what a loving noise four thousand people can make. There were flowers offstage for me, and the embarrassed Scala officials did not know what to do with them. Lorenzo picked them up and started to take them out himself until a Russian stagehand volunteered to do the job. Ivo Vinco was standing near Lorenzo, watch in hand; at the last curtain he turned to him and said, "Do you know how long that ovation was? Fifteen minutes!"

The success was tremendous and it was well reported in Russia. The critic I. Kozlovsky wrote in *Pravda*, September 10, 1964, a typical Russian response: "The most extraordinary thing in these presentations is Renata Scotto in the role of Lucia . . . she carries within her the vocal image of the character she creates. Every effect made on the audience is achieved through singing."

The *Lucia* success was not well reported at home, however; at least not in the news reports sent by Ghiringhelli to the Italian papers. He would have pictures taken with Freni and Cossotto and mention the rest of the run; from reading the Italian papers one might have thought that *Lucia di Lammermoor* had been canceled.

But the Russians were a different story. The demand for tickets was very high, and the Bolshoi Theater management asked me to sing a special recital at Tchaikovsky Hall in the Moscow Conservatory. There had been plans already for a Scala concert there that would include Birgit Nilsson, Freni, Simionato, and Giuseppe Taddei, but the Russians wanted a concert with me and for them I accepted immediately.

I sang seventeen bel canto arias, with Maestro Antonio Tonini at the piano, and in the intimacy of this hall I had one of my most unforgettable concert memories: the warmth of the public, the respect for the music, the lines of fans waiting to give me flowers all made up of people who had had to wait in lines longer still in the city in order to buy three carnations each. I had sung much of this country's music, and I wished I could come back sometime and sing it for them in their language. At the time I had sung in *Pique Dame, The Invisible City, Khovanshchina,* and *A Life for the Tsar;* and in London I had just heard Shostakovich's *Katerina Ismailova,* today rightfully restored to the composer's original title of *Lady Macbeth of Mtsensk,* and had been very moved by it. Whatever that public wanted I felt I had to give.

La Scala wanted something too, but I was not in a generous mood. Whatever joys I had in Moscow, they were not thanks to Ghiringhelli. So when they asked me to sing an extra *Lucia,* I simply told them that it was not in my contract and I wanted to go home. When I was told that the recital was not in the contract, I explained that I had sung that for this wonderful public but that was all. Giulietta Simionato waited until she got back to Milan to denounce Ghiringhelli and La Scala, on the front page of the *Corriere Lombardo* of September 30, 1964, for the "lamentable and countless outrages that some of our artists had to suffer in the hands of La Scala in Moscow," and she went on to tell reporters at the airport that she could understand why I refused to sing at La Scala again, because *Lucia* "was an immense personal success which was purposely minimized and denigrated for the Italian press."

For my part, I just sang my last *Lucia* and enjoyed the days I had left in Moscow. After the last performance the Minister of Culture brought a fan to my dressing room, the world's first cosmonaut, Yuri Gagarin, who was very shy; she then asked me and Lorenzo to meet with her the next day, which we did. The Bolshoi Theater wanted to engage me as a guest artist, and a contract was offered. This opportunity was rare for a Western artist then as now. But the money was not very good. And if I had to leave Italy in order to continue singing what and how I felt I had to sing, it was to the West and not the East that I would go.

Around the same time as this Bolshoi offer another one came, from the Metropolitan Opera in New York. I had a feeling that I would like the New York public too. So we managed to retrieve our passports from the Scala management at the last possible moment. Margherita Guglielmi sang the third *Lucia*, and Lorenzo and I left for Milan.

Three years later Ghiringhelli was replaced at La Scala, and I was ready to return. I was asked for a meeting but for some reason the management did not want it to take place in the theater. So we met with the new artistic director, Francesco Siciliani, at the Bristol Hotel, and he explained that La Scala wanted me back. They wanted me to sing the famous *Lucia* that I had taken to Moscow but had not sung in the house; and they offered anything else I might want that season. Now, there were several factors in my decision to return: the arrival of Francesco Siciliani; the discovery of Claudio Abbado, whom the critic Umberto Bonafini called the *deus ex machina* of the Milanese theatrical scene; and the growing influence of Gavazzeni, who would eventually become the real artistic director of La Scala.

We agreed to the *Lucia* and it was Lorenzo's idea to ask for a new production of Bellini's *I Capuleti e i Montecchi*, which I had done in Lisbon the previous year and in which the entrance aria *"Quante volte"* could mark my own return to the Scaligero stage. We insisted on a tenor Romeo, which would be the first time for the opera, because it would work better for my approach to the role; and we suggested Giacomo Aragall, the Spanish tenor who had everything one could want in Bellini's Romeo. The film director Renato Castellani was engaged to make his operatic debut with this production. Claudio Abbado would conduct both *Capuleti* and *Lucia*.

I Capuleti e i Montecchi has a libretto by Felice Romani, the author of *Norma*. The characters are of course deservedly best known from Shakespeare's Veronese lovers Romeo and Juliet, but even without Bellini's sublime music there would be something fascinating about this version: it dispenses with the Shakespearean drama and returns instead to the folk roots of this beautiful story. Capulet has called together his partisans to join him in what he fears will be an attack by the Montagues. Romeo has said that he will send an emissary to offer peace, but the old man recalls that Romeo is the cruel murderer of his only son, and the hatred for all the Montagues in general and for Romeo in particular mounts in the crowd. Tebaldo's forces have joined the Capulets, and the grateful father promises his daughter Juliet in marriage to Tebaldo if he will avenge his son. Friar Laurence, Juliet's confessor, warns Capulet that Juliet has been melancholy and sick, and that only by force can she be made to marry; but he is sent to Juliet with the message that she will do just that on that very same day. In the meantime Romeo has presented his plan for peace, which includes his betrothal to Juliet as a pledge of the end to violence in Verona. He is met with refusal and sings out, *"Ostinati, e tal sarà!"* as he readies himself again to wield his deadly sword.

Juliet waits alone in her rooms, dressed for a wedding

that she does not want. *"Eccomi in lieta veste . . . Siate, ah! siate per me faci ferali!"* She wishes her bridal gown were her funeral shroud. She thinks of Romeo but believes him far away, and her aria *"Oh quante volte, oh! quante ti chiedo al Ciel piangendo!"* establishes the musical tone for the opera, one of quiet desperation and unrealized strength in love. "How many times, how many," Juliet cries, "have I called out your name to heaven?" At this point in the libretto Juliet's confessor enters with the news that Romeo is not far away at all but is within the city walls and perhaps even in the palace. Soon she is with her lover again, but there is no lasting joy in their meeting; Juliet cannot bring herself to disobey her father's wishes even as Romeo begs her to run away with him and be happy. She begs him instead to go alone and escape the horrible dangers that face him. The last scene of Act I celebrates the wedding feast of Juliet and Tebaldo. Romeo is hidden among the guests and is bent on preventing the marriage at any cost; with him are several armed men in disguise. Trumpets ring out as they burst into the feast, and the party disperses into chaos. Juliet is left wondering what is to come of this sudden good fortune of not being forced to marry Tebaldo while at the same time she is terrified for Romeo. He enters and hurriedly reminds her of their love, once more begging her to run away with him. Tebaldo and Capulet find them, and again they are forced to part.

The war rages, and as Juliet worries over its outcome Friar Laurence appears with the news that at least Romeo is alive. He suggests a way out, the only way to avoid her marriage to Tebaldo: she must drink a potion that will bring on a sleep so deep that all will think she is dead. She hesitates before drinking, but only briefly. As her father enters to begin the wedding festivities once more, she appears to be mortally ill and is taken away as she sings, *"Pace ad un cor che muore . . ."*—not lying since part of her heart truly has died.

Romeo is desperate at not having yet received any news from Friar Laurence and goes looking for him. He finds Tebaldo and his men instead, but as they are about to begin another combat a funeral lament is heard that freezes both young men in their tracks. The funeral procession for Juliet passes by, and Romeo begs Tebaldo to kill him; Tebaldo cries that he himself is Juliet's killer and begs for death from Romeo instead.

In the final scene Romeo has entered the Capulet tombs. He cannot believe that Juliet is dead, so beautiful does she look even now. He bends over to kiss her lips but there is no life in the young woman. His last hope is poison. As he takes it, Juliet awakes and first thinks that Romeo is there as part of her confessor's plot. Her mistake is clear, however; Romeo is dying, and the girl, unable to live without him, falls dying too. The priest arrives with Capulet and his men in time to witness the tragedy but too late to help it, and Capulet throws himself on Juliet's body as Friar Laurence falls on Romeo.

The story of the opera is one that first appeared in print in Dante's *Inferno* and was later retold by Luigi da Porto in a sixteenth-century verse drama from which Romani wove his libretto in 1830. It was probably a true story, and soon became a favorite of troubadours. It was from Arthur Broke's poem that Shakespeare took it on and adapted it for his Globe Theater; it is interesting that the Shakespeare play was not popular in Italy, however, until after the resounding success of Bellini's opera in 1830.

At that premiere in Venice on March 11, 1830, the

lovers were played by two women, a soprano and a mezzo-soprano. Lorenzo and I realized as soon as I began studying the score, however, that if the right tenor could be found for the role of Romeo all of Bellini's music could be brought to life with an added dramatic integrity for today's audiences; one can always try to recreate the style and sensibility of the period, but it is impossible to recreate its ears, and too much academic fidelity can lead to bad theater. With Aragall we found the ideal Romeo, dashing and heroic and, most important, able to sing Bellini's music without alteration to the vocal line. And this we all did, for here as in *La Sonnambula, La Straniera, Norma,* as in all of Bellini in fact, the coloratura is so simple and so ravishing that the complicated fireworks that fashion has attached to his melodies become excessive once the original is heard.

Abbado's conducting, too, was impassioned and full of life but he never allowed the voices to fade into the background dramatically or musically. For this sensitivity to Bellini's and Donizetti's essentially vocal messages the Italian press compared him very favorably to his predecessor in *Lucia,* Herbert von Karajan. Renato Castellani's direction was brilliant for the production and a turning point in my career as well. I will return to him later, but I must say now that this man helped me a great deal in my awareness of my body onstage, in measuring my moves so that a single gesture could tell the tale of the whole evening. And yes, it is true that he tied my hands at the first rehearsal; I moved too much, and with him I learned to concentrate my actions and thus make them even clearer. The opera was a great success in Milan, and again in Montreal at Expo '67 when it became the hit of the World's Fair.

All this happened after my Metropolitan Opera debut in *Madama Butterfly* as well as my *Lucia* in Japan, the opera's first performance ever in that country; and my first *Madama Butterfly* at the Teatro Colón in Buenos Aires.

It was a beautiful time in my life, and by leaving my country and becoming successful in other countries it seemed that I had made it possible to return on my terms and no longer sing in the way that tradition demanded but in the way I knew I had to sing, the way that felt honest, satisfying. In my way. With bel canto, this meant figures of flesh and blood drawn within the correct musical lines: the drama and the music are inseparable. I would work out all ornamentations, when they were indicated, with Lorenzo at home as we prepared each role, always in the style of the music and always simple and close to the words being sung. There is nothing wrong with sheer display, but opera can be so much more. And that is the way we did that 1968 *Lucia di Lammermoor,* with Abbado again conducting and Giorgio de Lullo directing, with gorgeous sets and costumes by Pier Luigi Pizzi.

By this time I knew the woman Lucia very well. I sang her the way I would sing her again in New York at the Met; I remember I even came close to talking Abbado into cutting all the interpolations into the vocal line altogether, including the duet with the flute and all the unwritten high notes, but in the end he was afraid of the management and we agreed to leave much of it in. "Lucia is a real woman at last," read one headline. "Renata di Lammermoor" proclaimed another. As the New York *World-Telegram* later wrote, for the audience it was "Renata di Savona." They were not wrong: it was impossible for me to separate the tragedienne from the tragedy, the singer from the song on that beautiful opening night in 1967.

After *Lucia* I prepared two more bel canto roles: *Maria di Rohan* for La Scala, although for the happiest of reasons I had to delay singing this opera a few years—I was pregnant; and Meyerbeer's *Roberto il diavolo*, the first of the two Meyerbeer operas that I have sung.

I did sing the *Maria di Rohan* first in Lisbon in 1968, just after the Scala *Capuleti* and *Lucia;* and later with Gavazzeni at La Fenice in 1974. It is the most interesting of Donizetti's four Marias, the second to last of his operas, and a fascinating musical portrait. It premiered the same year as Verdi's *I Lombardi*, and the thunder of a new age of music is not far from this Donizetti score: the rhythms of the music and the drama are one, when sung well; and as the opera progresses one can hear even within scenes how Donizetti began to move away from a succession of solo numbers to new musical forms that express each character's conflicts in direct, ineffably romantic ways. Maria's final outburst is a simple, exposed lament in B-flat that is one of Donizetti's most precious gems; it is one of his last works and the master was in full command. It is also a great dramatic bel canto heroine, not a coloratura role at all, and singing it helped me to find new dramatic meanings within the musicality of bel canto; the score begged not to be changed by a singer, it commanded respect. By the Venice production I was ready to sing bel canto this way, and I found in *Maria di Rohan* a close musical relative of Verdi's *Un ballo in maschera*.

I had enjoyed *Elisir* and *Don Pasquale* for different reasons, but I found that *Maria di Rohan*, together with *Lucia di Lammermoor* and *Anna Bolena*, are the most innovative, profound, and beautiful of Donizetti's operas. Beyond

these, the Donizetti operas that have come to my attention
have not captured my imagination. Donizetti is not Bellini; all of Bellini's operas are truly great, profoundly dramatic music. (The only Bellini operas I have not sung are
Beatrice di Tenda and *Bianca e Fernando.*) But Donizetti's
Maria di Rohan is a profound piece, fascinating in musical
and dramatic terms. It is very much a work that deserves
to be restored to the repertory, much more so than many
of the other Donizetti operas that have been resuscitated
by the recently awakened interest in bel canto.

Meyerbeer's *Roberto il diavolo* was a compromise, even
if it was a beautiful one. I sang it for the opening of the
Maggio Musicale Fiorentino on May 7, 1968, with Maestro
Nino Sanzogno conducting and Boris Christoff in the role
of Bertramo. Margherita Wallmann directed and the stark
sets were by Josef Svoboda, whose fabulous *Vespri* I would
later sing at the Met. The fourth-act duet alone, where the
harp and the voices seem to rise together to the heavens,
would be reason enough to do this very grand opera.

I also did many things then that I would not do today.
As with Rossini, Meyerbeer's music invites improvisation,
so my sins were not mortal. But I confess that I changed
the written cadenza, taking a high C, then an E natural
after the cabaletta, all for vocal effect. The audience went
crazy and I received some of the most beautiful applause
of my career. We all sang well, and the production was
strong, but the reason that I look at *Roberto il diavolo* as less
than a high and honest moment in my career is partly that
it was *Roberto il diavolo* and not *Robert le diable.* It is of
course sometimes desirable to sing in the language of the
audience, but I have grown to prefer to make the audience
understand the language of the composer, and I have tried
to do only that in my mature career as an artist. Also, the

five acts were cut drastically. All of Isabella's music remained, I saw to that. But the maestro agreed to cuts in everyone else's parts, sometimes within scenes and other times within actual numbers. I do not think that it gave a fair image of what Meyerbeer wanted. Fairness to Meyerbeer was years later, in New York, when I sang the rule of Berthe in *Le Prophète*. That was truly Meyerbeer opera.

And what else was I singing? I was no longer being told that Puccini was wrong for me, imagine that. And of course I stayed with my first love, Violetta. She led me back to Verdi again and again. And Verdi each time made me think and rethink opera.

Six

Opera Is Verdi

My musical life began with Verdi. It was *Rigoletto* that first taught me the magic that I have never ceased to find on-stage, since that first time that my uncle Salvatore took me to see Tito Gobbi as Verdi's tragic hunchback on my first trip to Milan. It was *La Traviata* that first introduced me to the public, that huge personage that would be only next to my family in my affection. And it was Verdi more than any other composer whom I thought of when I thought of opera: vocal technique and acting alike, I felt that I could learn it all from this master.

In the earlier days when I was faced with the problem of being labeled as a light soprano when I knew better, I had to find a way to make the public see what I really could do. I tried to sing each role not as tradition suggested but as the score demanded and, seen in this light, the music of Verdi did not seem to call for light or dramatic or coloratura, rather it called for singers, simply singers who could produce his notes and remain faithful to his drama. If I could do this, I could sing any Verdi role. But how could I find out? Was there a role that convinced theaters and audiences that I could move to what they thought of as the more dramatic repertory? Yes, there were a few such roles along the way. *La Straniera* of Bellini led the way to *Norma*. *A Life for the Tsar* opened the doors for many Puccini roles. And *I Lombardi* reassured me that I could sing Verdi whenever I felt that it was right for me to do so. At the time, however, I did not look at each preparation as a hurdle or landmark in my career, I simply sang. I did not set out to produce a different voice for Giselda in *I Lombardi* any more than I became the new

Toti Dal Monte, as some earlier critics insisted on compli-
menting me, when I sang Gilda in *Rigoletto*.

I remember a *Rigoletto* at La Fenice in 1960, just after
Lorenzo and I were married. I had already recorded the
role by this time and had sung it enough to feel that I
knew Gilda very well. She was young and innocent, but
she was a woman, not a doll. Toti Dal Monte lived in
Venice, and she came to the performance with a group of
her students and friends. Ordinarily visitors do not go
backstage during a performance; rather, they wait until
the end of the opera to visit the singers. But of course an
exception had to be made when an illustrious prima donna
like Toti Dal Monte said that she wanted to come to my
dressing room after the curtain fell on Act I. Now, even
good comments can be a distraction in the middle of a
performance; but I was really thrilled to meet this great
singer when she came into my dressing room with her
friends as I prepared for Act II.

"Ah, bella, bellissima," she said, "but, my dear, this is
not the way to sing Gilda."

I smiled and held on to the makeup case, a little
stunned. She went on.

"This is not Gilda, you are not Gilda, this is not
Verdi's young girl. You play her like a woman. You sing
like a dramatic soprano, too dramatic. And where are your
long blond braids? All Gildas have to have long blond
braids."

Then came the best part.

"You should sing Gilda the way I sang it. My days
were the days of the true Gilda. If you like I will find time
while you are here to give you some lessons."

All of this from a singer to another singer, at a time
when, minutes before curtain, everyone knows that it is

not the best of occasions to bring up the need for vocal lessons. And I was not a student in 1960. I could not believe all that I had just heard and for once I had nothing to say. I had a performance to continue.

Lorenzo spoke for me. He stood between me and the Venetian diva and said, "*Madama,* if my wife were to sing Gilda the way it was done in your day, I would not let her step on that stage today."

Toti Dal Monte was furious; she turned pale and left as her shocked coterie muttered, "How can you do this to the great Toti Dal Monte? How can you?" Soon everyone in Venice was asking the same question. Many people suggested that I apologize to the diva, that she was just very old. I said that age is no excuse for lack of consideration, that no matter what she thought of my singing she might have waited until after the performance to pay me that strange visit. She was the one who needed to apologize to me.

Finally a brave music lover gave a dinner party toward the end of the *Rigoletto* run and invited both of us. She did not apologize to me, I did not apologize to her. But sometime during dinner we caught each other smiling knowingly, each out of the corner of her eye. And we became very friendly after that night in Venice.

Early in my career I had sung only roles that fell into Toti Dal Monte's repertory, so many people compared me to her; they compared me to many singers, actually, in that desire to label before accepting that is especially strong in Italy. If any comparison pleased me, it was that to Mafalda Favero, the great and underestimated Italian soprano. But I never copied her. I copied no one. A great career is not made of imitation, and from the very beginning I resolved to be among the very best or not to sing at all. I needed to be myself. But in Italy, unless you are singing a world premiere, you are always categorized according to your predecessors. It was very stifling to be told of the way Dal Monte did things, the way Tebaldi did things, the way Callas did things. In the 1960s my career became international, with New York, Buenos Aires, and Tokyo following Moscow, Berlin, London, and many others. Finding a completely new audience gave me the complete freedom to take risks, to choose. After ten years I had earned the freedom to be myself.

But earning that freedom was very important, and I think that I needed those years of fighting tradition and of slow growth in order to realize my full potential at the right time. Many young singers today lack the patience for that fight and take short cuts to a major career; it is a mistake. Traveling too soon from theater to theater in country to country too early in one's life can give you worse than jet lag. Many become singing machines of the familiar international style, which is no style at all, sounding the same in *Luisa Miller* and *Macbeth* or *Traviata*, using up all their resources in ten years. Some try this without a proper technical base, and they are finished even sooner and left with no voice at all. The biggest loss perhaps is the loss of responsibility to the music. A singer has to have time to think about what she is doing and she must do it with the belief that it is indeed a great thing, that a voice is a great gift. To give one's life for a great art—and this is what singing opera should be—imposes a tremendous burden; it implies letting the voice and the brain work together and never stop working to create something that remains behind, the living memory of great music. I am as glad for my ten years of waiting and singing in Italy as I am for knowing when I had to break out and take new risks.

And I do take risks. I need them. My first *Vespri siciliani* was a risk, so was my first *Lombardi*, both when I was told it was too soon but Lorenzo and I knew that the time was right. And in each case it was my singing of Verdi in other roles that had made me grow to these new challenges.

I sang *Rigoletto* everywhere and recorded it twice in the studio. The first was with Bastianini as my father and Kraus as my lover; Gavazzeni conducted. The second won me a Grand Prix du Disque not long after Dal Monte told me that I was not Gilda. Dietrich Fischer-Dieskau sang the hunchback and Carlo Bergonzi was the Duke: Rafael Kubelik conducted. When I have recorded a role twice I have shown a new side of the character each time, and with the exception of my first *Bohème* I am very pleased with each version. This is true of *Rigoletto*, even though I prefer the first with Bastianini, Kraus, and Gavazzeni. It was unusual working with Fischer-Dieskau on this opera; he sang everything so correctly, in such a cool, classical manner. The overall interpretation was more purely musical than dramatic, and it affected my Gilda. It was in some ways an artistic achievement of a very high level, but I know that Verdi's stature comes from his earthiness, his humanity. With Kubelik and Fischer-Dieskau I made a beautifully musical portrait of Gilda. I think that with Gavazzeni and Bastianini I put on records what I like to give in the theater: a true operatic performance.

I learned around this time that in every score Verdi asks for a soprano, not for a lyric, or a spinto, or a dramatic. Just a soprano, with a long tessitura and every technical difficulty imaginable. What the composer demands is that the singer treat the voice exactly as an instrument, that she play it. Verdi's is the most demanding music I have ever sung, and the most meaningful to me. In Verdi, the words and the music are implied in the vocal technique he demands, and what he calls for is a complete singer.

Sometimes in recordings the musical values can outweigh the drama, much as happens in arias in recital as opposed to within their operatic context. One unusual Verdi heroine for me is *Aida*, whom I do not want to sing but whose arias I like in concert. I recorded *"Qui Radames verrà . . . O patria mia"* with the Monte Carlo Opera during this period of transition to new Verdi roles, and the record pleases me very much. I can hear the technique that Llopart taught me, how important bel canto is for singing Verdi and verismo. I can hear it in Kraus's Duke and Alfredo Germont in our *Rigoletto* and *La Traviata* recordings.

Alfredo Kraus and I grew up together as singers; we had the same teacher and we have the same technique. He chose to remain a pure *belcantista* and a Verdian, while I chose to expand my repertory into the verismo period. But the choice is one of congeniality of theatrical expression; the technique is the same. The key is in the art of portamento and legato. Some singers overdo the first and ignore the second; that is in fact one of the marks of the international sound one hears in many opera houses. A portamento should be the loving act of carrying the voice from one note to another; legato hides the act in smooth discretion. Callas knew how to use portamento with art, but many singers who think they follow in her path misunderstand the concept and turn portamento into glissando, lazy and rude. Falling into too much portamento is easiest for the lazy singer.

When Mercedes Llopart taught me she made it easy. Like so much else in a singer's technical repertory, legato and portamento could be understood while singing Bellini. Take, for example, *"Ah! non credea mirarti."* That has everything. For example, listen to the first phrase and notice how easy it would be to turn the syllables *"arti"* into a lazy glissando on each note; I have heard it done that way, each note drooping and scooping beyond Bellini's score. Now look at the score and notice how it tells exactly how to join each note with legato, smoothly and without exaggeration. In matters of interpretation, the best advice comes from the score.

When making records I prefer to divide the sessions into very long takes; it is not at all tiring. It is rather closer to the feeling one gets in the theater, and the recordings show it. Even when there may be a few imperfect notes, long takes (and live recordings, when they are well made) reflect the excitement of a performance. That is the way my records with Lorin Maazel, James Levine, and Riccardo Muti are made, and I love it. The microphone becomes an imaginary public then, a combination of New York, Milan, Bonn, and London. My two *Traviata* recordings trace my relationship with that public and my growth with Verdi; they are twenty years apart, and I am very pleased with both. I had sung *La Traviata* everywhere. Even before my 1965 Metropolitan Opera debut in *Madama Butterfly* I was in Verona until the end of summer singing *La Traviata* in front of thirty thousand people (a Verona record) in a production directed by Mauro Bolognini. Then came my hundredth Violetta, on March 30, 1967, at the Metropolitan Opera. It was a long way from that first *Traviata* when a teenager struggled on Christmas Eve to bring something of herself to Verdi's most beautiful heroine. And on that night in New York when I sang my hundredth *Traviata* I remembered one of the headlines from *La Notte,* July 4, 1953: *"Con la voce di Renata è rinata La Traviata"*

It was a generous thing to say to me then, and I think I have lived up to that estimation. And not only do I feel Violetta's rebirth each time I sing the role, I myself am renewed as a singer by Verdi's music. I trust it and love it more each time I return to his scores. My two Violettas on record show this growth. Unlike the commercial *Rigoletto* recordings, both of the *Traviatas* were conducted by Italians, by great Verdians: the first in 1960 with Antonino Votto, whose Verdian lineage can be traced through Toscanini to Verdi himself; the second in 1980 with Riccardo Muti, a pupil of Votto and the continuer of that great Verdi tradition. In the first the men in Violetta's life were Gianni Raimondi and Ettore Bastianini. In the second they were Alfredo Kraus and Renato Bruson. Both recordings make me very happy. The first I made when I was still living in Italy, steeped in the traditions of the Italian theater and doing my best within those boundaries. The score was cut, and with what remained I interpolated high notes everywhere. Maestro Votto had me come to his house every day for three weeks before the recording began, teaching me the role all over again, note by note, showing me the way to find fresh meanings very much within his rich musical tradition. I was fortunate that the music is so sublime and that I could sing it, because the words would become more important only later when the score became more important and sacred for me. Still, it is a record that makes a good case for that tradition and it explains why none of us suffered terribly much when we were forced to sing this way: the performance is very exciting. In the 1970s the great film and stage director Mauro Bolognini revealed to me the vast universe of Violetta's dramatic possibilities. By the time I came to work with Riccardo Muti I knew Verdi much better, and I was fortunate to find colleagues who had reached the same conclusions as I: after so many *Traviatas* it was time to give the public something else, and in this case that meant going back to the score and nowhere else, singing every note that Verdi wrote and following his every wish. My portrayal now was perhaps more intimate and more intense: to communicate simply and directly the sublimation of a love through the most extreme sacrifice. So, for example, a moment like *"Dite alla giovine"* was a pivotal point in Violetta's sacrifice. This pure and young girl is everything that Violetta is not, but at this moment Violetta has everything and gives up everything for her sake. It is not that the voice was any different; rather, it was my interpretation, my singing, that changed as my Violetta changed. Perhaps the second recording will one day be considered part of another old tradition; for now I believe that the approach that I took is the most valid way of presenting *La Traviata* today.

And it was by never abandoning that opera that I began to realize over the years the possibilities of other Verdi scores. We studied *I Lombardi*, considered much more dramatic than my usual repertory, and I saw that the traditional vocal categories were meaningless and that I could bring something beautiful to this score. It had not been revived in Italy for more than thirty years.

I Lombardi was Verdi's fourth opera, following the success of *Nabucco* and becoming almost as much of a triumph for the composer at the Scala premiere on February 11, 1843. It was the first Verdi opera to be heard in New York, and it was a particular pleasure for me to sing it in concert at Carnegie Hall. But the fabulous evening for me was in Rome. The first act is a story of revenge. In the early eleventh century in Milan, the two sons of Lord Folco are in love with the same girl, named Viclinda. When she chooses Arvino over Pagano, the rejected brother attacks Arvino and wounds him. Then he runs away to the Holy Land. When he returns he kneels in front of St. Ambrogio and asks his brother's forgiveness, which he receives. In fact Pagano plans a cruel revenge by burning down the house where his brother and his wife and their young daughter Giselda are asleep. It is Giselda who dominates the opera from this point. She keeps the two brothers from killing each other and she is later captured near a cave in the Holy Land only to fall in love with the son of her captor, whom she converts to Christianity and eventually baptizes. Once she thinks him dead but he turns out to be alive and disguised as a crusader. The last scene shows dawn behind the holy city of Jerusalem, as a hymn to God is sung by Giselda and the crusaders.

The music is energetic and brilliant, containing much of what was to come later in Verdi. My favorite section is Giselda's *"Salve, Maria"* from Act II; she is so close to another Verdi heroine, Desdemona. Giselda's visions hark back to *Nabucco* but with a sweeter edge. If Violetta can be said to require every skill in a soprano's repertory, the same can almost be said of Giselda.

On November 20, 1969, we opened at the Rome Opera, with Gianandrea Gavazzeni conducting and the great Verdian Ruggero Raimondi as the evil Pagano. It was a triumph that gave me particular satisfaction because it meant that I was now free to expand my repertory in any direction I wished. I must repeat what Maestro Gavazzeni wrote in a letter:

> The subdivisions of vocal categories for operatic singers are mere conventions that do not correspond to reality. Light, lyric, dramatic: definitions of convenience. So you see that the light and lyric Scotto proved herself ready for *Butterfly, I Vespri Siciliani, Ballo* (all under my direction) as well as *Luisa Miller* and *Trovatore*. For where there is true love of music, there is a refusal of the static, a need for new challenges, of other experiences. It is a matter of eluding and transcending all conventional limits. It is always a matter of self-discipline and intelligence. And here lies the interest and the worth of Renata Scotto's new phase: in the rich patrimony of the past, and in the passion for new characters and diverse musical substance.

With such encouragement from colleagues, with Verdi in my voice and Malibran always in my heart, I will go on singing, I will go on growing. *Grazie, maestro.*

Seven

Madama Butterfly and
the Bing Bondage

Since 1960, when I made my debut in the United States with the Chicago Lyric Opera in *La Bohème,* I had sung in Dallas, Miami, Pittsburgh, Washington, and of course again in Chicago. I had not sung in New York and did not think very much about that fact. Outside of Italy my favorite city was London and my favorite theater Covent Garden, where for years I sang as much as I did anywhere at home. The British public, which had been so good to me in that Edinburgh Festival years before, became as a loving friend, and to that public I returned as Lucia, Gilda, Amina, Adina, Mimi, Butterfly, Manon, and always Violetta. It was the Royal Opera that let me sing Violetta when La Scala refused me.

In London one of my most beautiful dreams came true: I sang Gilda to Tito Gobbi's Rigoletto. It was a live opera broadcast for the BBC, and I was awed. There I sat next to the man who had inspired me to become a singer, and as he sang to me ". . . *piangi, piangi, fanciulla"* I cried real tears. I could hardly believe that this was real, I could not get that Christmas in Savona out of my mind, and I was very, very happy.

I particularly liked giving recitals in England, and I remember fondly my debut at the Royal Albert Hall in 1966, one of those very operatic recitals filled with Bellini and Verdi arias, but also including songs from Scarlatti to Tosti. What made it memorable for me was that through it all I was accompanied for the first time by Gerald Moore, a pianist who played with a conductor's gift for listening and guiding at once. Traveling to work in different countries is never a hardship when I am so lucky as to find colleagues like that.

Earlier, when I was in Moscow, we received word of an offer from the Metropolitan Opera in New York to sing in *Madama Butterfly, Lucia di Lammermoor,* and *L'elisir d'amore* in the 1965–66 season, with a similar offer for the following season. I accepted, choosing the Met's offer over the Bolshoi Opera's surprise contract that I had been shown after the Moscow *Lucia* with La Scala.

If Verdi is the most important opera composer, the master of bel canto, Puccini is the only great verismo composer. *Madama Butterfly* is his greatest opera and it is my favorite. I sang it first in Savona just after my operatic debut and, as with Violetta, I have grown with Cio-Cio-San over the last thirty years. I learned to approach Puccini's score with the same respect that I approach Verdi's or Bellini's music, to master note by note, to live with the libretto until the necessary and only way to say those words is in the composer's notes. Then I find something new every time I sing.

Most of all I learned very soon that Butterfly is not a doll, as she used to be sung so often: she is a woman, she says so. Here is someone who had to face poverty, shame, and the death of her father, who was made to go with men when she was only a child. Someone who has lived, so much and so sadly. In Act I she sings that she is only fifteen but already old. When she meets Pinkerton she is happy, but what kind of happiness is hers? She is desperate, controlled in her behavior but anxious in her speech; she keeps repeating how happy she is because by saying it to herself again and again she hopes to believe it. From her entrance Butterfly must show this to the audience, she must never be a cute Japanese doll. Her private conversations with Pinkerton in the first act must be clearly private, for she is very much afraid of everything around her, of the life that has hurt her so much and which she might escape now thanks to this man. She must almost whisper to Pinkerton the news that she has adopted his faith—*"Ieri son salita tutta sola in segreto alla Missione"*—because if Butterfly's relatives hear her they will be angry and perhaps ruin this beautiful dream. Then she must be sensuous and sing delicately, caressed by the pianissimi winds and gentle soft strings, announcing that she must follow her destiny: *"Io seguo il mio destino."* It should be a womanly sound that fills out that long legato line; it is free and effortless and reveals her character so completely that Sharpless, the only man who understands Butterfly, warns Pinkerton to be careful not to betray her trust. When the newlyweds are left alone, Butterfly is again afraid, not of Pinkerton but of the evening's end; it has been so beautiful. She cannot believe it—she is afraid to go inside, afraid to lose the moment, one of the few truly happy moments of her hard life. She is only fifteen years old.

In Act II she is eighteen and more desperate, singing of her happiness with profound sadness and of hope with no hope at all. With *"Un bel dì"* she almost believes her words, she gives herself hope by repeating that yes, yes, he will come back, he will come back. She becomes a phoenix and rises above the cruelty of her situation. Her whole life is in this aria, and Puccini was very specific about exactly how to sing it. It begins *da lontano*, with a distant thread of voice that paints the image of the day when the ship will come back to the harbor. She imagines that whole day, where she will be, what she will do; she begins to believe, in desperation she talks herself into hope once more. At the high B-flat that announces her renewed faith, she really must sound as if *"con sicura fede l'aspetto."* Her faith is unshakable. When Sharpless confronts her with the possibility that Pinkerton may not return and asks her what she might do then, she replies very simply, "Two things I might do: go back to entertaining men, or better, die." In Act III all is lost when Butterfly sees Pinkerton's wife in the garden. They can have the child, they can take anything, there is nothing but death left for her. *"Tu, tu, piccolo Iddio!"* is the strongest scene in the opera, and one that always affects me almost too much. There is great danger for a singer in allowing sentiment to interfere with the craft. One should always be in control of the emotions in order to be able to control the music; that is, Butterfly cannot literally cry, just as the soprano who actually goes mad in Lucia will probably sing off key. But there are certain moments in opera when I find myself with real tears running down my cheeks: sometimes at the end of *Manon Lescaut,* always when I sing *"Amami, Alfredo."* And always at the death of Butterfly.

It is one role that I sang instinctively at the beginning but with which I had great sympathy even before I began to study it; today I understand it better than ever because I have children of my own, and that has added a profound new dimension to my dramatic understanding. To be a mother has helped me to realize every role.

I recorded *Madama Butterfly* twice because I have never stopped growing with the role; both were done with great conductors, and if I prefer the second recording it is probably because I can hear the difference that having children made to my interpretation. It is my favorite Puccini opera, and it was Puccini's favorite as well.

I was thrilled to make it my debut with the Metropolitan Opera on October 13, 1965. It was an unforgettable night. I instantly liked that public. As a matter of fact, when a critic wrote that "It was love at first sight between Miss Scotto and the New York public," he was telling the absolute truth. All the reviews were good. *The New Yorker* said that "She is a singer of extreme refinement, who knows the value of a well-placed pianissimo and who can express a great variety of psychological shades of meaning by subtly coloring her tone." The New York *Herald Tribune* wrote that it "was an occasion for rejoicing, and there was plenty of it in the form of applause and welcoming shouts to the new artist who, above all, is distinctly an individual." The New York *Times* managed to slip in that I reminded one of Toti Dal Monte, but it was meant as a compliment. The October 14 review went on to say,

> Her Butterfly was a combination of Japanese grace and Italian volatility, emotions flying through her body and across her face with seeming spontaneity. Tenderness, sorrow, anger succeeded each other quickly and convincingly in movement, expression and vocal coloration, so that one became totally immersed in the pathetic tragedy of Puccini's heroine. . . . It was a measure of Miss Scotto's sincerity that she refused to step out of character during the long ovation that greeted her singing of the "Un bel dì" aria, although it must have been tempting to the debutante to acknowledge the shouting from the audience.

As soon as I arrived at the Metropolitan Opera I met Francis Robinson, and he made me feel at home. If ever I needed advice, if I needed to discuss a problem, if I was lonely, it was not Mr. Bing but Francis Robinson who was there for me as for so many other singers. He loved music and he loved singers; he was the Metropolitan Opera's best friend. His death was a great loss, an irreplaceable loss to the Met. For the last few years I have relied on Larry Riederman, a friend and adviser, and an administrator of whom Francis Robinson would have approved.

After that first *Butterfly* the Metropolitan was never far from my heart. That same season I sang Lucia and Adina, and in the new house I sang Violetta and Amina. It became my home. And, as in every home, things were not always happy.

I knew from experience that the way to keep my favorite roles growing and fresh was to keep singing new roles as well. It is good for the audience to see an artist in a new light, and it is good for the performer to be challenged. In the controversy that followed, I never for a moment stopped adoring the roles of Butterfly, Lucia, Adina, and Violetta. But the following year the Met gave me Butterfly, Lucia, Adina, and Violetta; then Rudolf Bing offered me Butterfly, Lucia, Adina, and Violetta. And for still another season the offer read Butterfly, Lucia, Adina, and Violetta.

It is not so unforgivable that I wanted something else. I expected that my Met debut would lead to opportunities for growth, to new challenges. In the beginning I was afraid to say anything to Mr. Bing, the Met's general manager. He was not a man who inspired confidence. I felt timid around him, not in the sense of being afraid to talk but simply feeling that if I said anything I might bother him. He was not someone to take to lunch to have a nice talk. Finally, after three years at the Met, it was time again for negotiating a contract. He offered me Butterfly, Lucia, Adina, and Violetta.

I remember that I told him, "Mr. Bing, I am very happy to be here, but I would like the opportunity to sing some new roles, perhaps a new production. After three seasons I think that I am entitled to a new production." I reminded him of the great success that I had had in the house and said that it would be even better if my public could see me in something new.

"Sorry, miss, you'll have to wait your turn."

That was all he said.

So I answered, "Fine, Mr. Bing, I'll wait until you call me back." There was no fight or any further discussion, I just left New York after the remaining commitments ran out in the next two seasons. I was sorry. I loved the theater and still do, and Lorenzo and I had bought a home just outside New York. But I was tired of hearing the wonderful compliments of *"Brava, bravissima,"* followed by nothing. At this point I had had ten new productions at La Scala and two opening nights; the Met should not do any less. It was not that I craved the honor of new productions but that I needed to sing new roles in order to keep the old ones fresh and in order to continue to grow as a singer.

The press is fond of exaggerating the temperament of singers, and the New York *Times* headline of "If the Met Won't Sing Her Tune, It's Goodbye Scotto," was typical. But this was no grandstand play, no controversy. I was just honest. And I did not need to hang around and wait my turn. When the Met eventually called me back, it was for Verdi's *I vespri siciliani,* and I was asked very timidly if I would consider returning to New York. I answered immediately, "Of course, it's not *Lucia.*"

But this was under a new management, and the atmosphere in the theater was quite different. Still, I agreed to return not because Bing had left but rather because I was offered something new, and I was glad to do it. For me the change in management did not affect the way I work in the theater. I still go to the first rehearsal and stay through the last, I sing, and I go home; I have never been very interested in backstage politics. At the Met I still have to ask where some offices are. But the change in management did change how good I feel about my work in the theater. Anthony Bliss and James Levine have been great, and I will speak more about them later. When Maestro Levine has new ideas he calls me directly and we discuss them; I do the same thing. That is how we did *Manon Lescaut*, and that is also how we came up with the ideas for productions of *Macbeth*, *Francesca da Rimini*, and *La clemenza di Tito*. More than a maestro, he is the ideal colleague and friend.

Whether working with good colleagues or dealing with a Bing, the two most important roles of my life soon gave me a completely new outlook not only on my career but on everything. And they are roles I never sang.

First there was Rossini's *L'assedio di Corinto* at La Scala, which along with *Maria di Rohan* were to be my Milan roles in 1968–69. Instead I had my first child, my daughter Laura, on May 31, 1969. My sister Luciana was the godmother; and my brother-in-law Oppilio was the godfather. I eventually sang *Maria di Rohan*, in that production, in fact; but I never returned to *L'Assedio*, and I consider it one of my two most important roles.

The other is Verdi's *Giovanna d'Arco*, an opera about one of my favorite heroines in history. Instead I had my favorite hero, my son Filippo, on June 21, 1972. His godparents were our good friends the bass Paolo Washington

Preceding page, my debut at La Scala in *La Wally,* in the role of Walter. I am wearing a false nose because the director thought mine was too small; after opening night I noticed that it was not the nose they were applauding, so I just wore my own. (photo: Piccagliani, La Scala) At top, *Lucia di Lammermoor* curtain call at La Scala with the conductor Claudio Abbado. (photo: Piccagliani, La Scala) Bottom, Verdi's *Luisa Miller* in Catania. (photo: Giovanni Consoli)

Opposite page, top left, as Gretel, with the mezzo-soprano Fiorenza Cossotto, playing my older brother in Humperdinck's *Hansel and Gretel.* (photo: Piccagliani, La Scala) Top right, *Lucia di Lammermoor* in Budapest. (photo: Kertesz Gyula) Bottom, as Juliet in Bellini's *I Capuleti e i Montecchi,* with tenor Giacomo Aragall as Romeo. (photo: Piccagliani, La Scala)

Opposite page, Cio-Cio-San, the role of my Metropolitan Opera debut in 1965. The *Herald Tribune* reported that "it was love at first sight between Miss Scotto and the New York audience." Suor Angelica in Puccini's *Il Trittico* at the Met. While preparing the role I recalled my own days in the Canossian convent in Milan. (photos: J. Heffernan, Metropolitan Opera)

Mimi in Puccini's *La Bohème,* one of the most beautiful roles I have sung. Opposite page, seducing Plácido Domingo in *Manon Lescaut.*

Following page, Elena in *I vespri siciliani* by Verdi, marking my return to the Met in 1972. (photos: J. Heffernan)

and the soprano Ilva Ligabue. I never sang Verdi's Giovanna, and she is the other most important role in my career.

And I mean this in a very real sense. I am a better singer for having become a mother. If this sounds like a cliché, so be it; perhaps maturity lies precisely in understanding for the first time the profound truth of just such a cliché. I understood everything in music and in life so much better. Before Laura and Filippo of course I was very happy, and Lorenzo made me happier each day. But I still had a touch of the little girl from Savona who did not go out of the convent and lived only for music. Now I cannot say that I live for music, I live for life. I used to be so affected by everything that happened to me, cry over everything, get so excited; when I had a child all those things from the theater seemed so small. I realized what is really important. If tenors could be mothers they would not be the way they are.

Lorenzo and I waited nine years to have children for the sake of my career, which was then the most important thing in my life. Now it is only a part, not the biggest. Life itself is what is important, my family. My career makes me who I am, but it is not everything. Now I understand how to listen much better because of listening to my children. I began to look at their lives and at the world around me, at everyday problems. So when I go onstage now I can reflect life better in my work. And after all that is why people go to cry at *Bohème* or *Butterfly;* they see their own feelings onstage, but far away. That, I learned, is the very human genius of Puccini: to have put life onstage, real life. Think of how many children were left behind by their fathers during the war, how many Butterflies perhaps had to live and cope as well as they could, or perhaps they too killed themselves. In Puccini these images are brutal, they are from real life; and knowing this is the key to portraying a verismo character. I could not have reached this understanding without my having a family of my own.

The biggest decision that a man can make is to give up his own career to dedicate himself to his wife's. That is what Lorenzo did. People see me onstage and I am famous, but nobody sees Lorenzo, so they do not know how important he is. How many times he has been called Mr. Scotto and he does not get angry, although I get furious. And how many times I have realized that without him I would not be where I am or who I am, that every decision in my career has been made with him. His head for business lets him handle my affairs as well as all his real estate and other business ventures. His ear for music and his musical sensibility are the guideposts for my operatic decisions, from the roles I sing to the selections I include in recital. And his patience and consideration, knowing when to wait and when to comfort me. We decide everything together, and Laura and Filippo were our happiest decisions.

Eight

I Vespri Callasiani

Opera was not born with Maria Callas, and it did not die with her death. Opera did not die with the death of Malibran or Ponselle. It will not die when I am gone. It lives on, as it must, in new voices. Callas may well be a beautiful memory against which many great sopranos will be measured, but each artist has her time. Callas had hers then, before mine. The competition and polemics were imagined and perpetuated by sick fanatics.

When La Scala offered me the opening night's new 1970 production of *I vespri siciliani*, I was ecstatic. After *I Lombardi* I was eager to face a new Verdi challenge and the opera seemed an ideal one. For the opening Maria Callas was coming from Paris, where she lived then in retirement; she had not sung at La Scala since the 1962 *Medea* and I had not seen her since I worked on the recording of that opera in 1957. Still, I admired her then as much as before; and I was pleased that she would be in the first box on opening night. I had never had any trouble with her fans before, no trouble with claques at all as a matter of fact. And of course I did not expect any trouble from these groups at La Scala. One would have to reach very far to imagine a competition between a singer in *Vespri* in 1970 and a retired singer who had sung it in 1951. Apparently someone wanted to reach that far, and it was not a very nice experience.

Verdi's *I vespri siciliani* began life as *Les vêpres siciliennes*, commissioned for the opening of the Paris Exposition in 1855. It is a vast patriotic tapestry in five acts, with the plot being of less importance than the passions and music of the principal characters. Based on a true tale of the occupation of Sicily by the French in the thirteenth century, the opera finds Verdi writing about Italy not only of that century but of always. "What happened in Sicily in the thirteenth century happened again in all of Italy in the Risorgimento," said Maestro Gavazzeni; and it was in that period that La Scala set its production by Giorgio de Lullo, designed by Pier Luigi Pizzi, for this 1970–71 season.

The climax of the opera is the massacre that Wagner misunderstood as a silly "night of carnage" when the French soldiers are caught off guard and killed to the last man by the Sicilian patriots after the signal has been given to begin the killings through the vesper bells that announce the wedding of Elena, a Sicilian, to Arrigo, a Frenchman.

Elena's music is unmistakably Italian, no matter what the period of the production might be; she is a great Verdi woman. Her first scene includes her singing on a dare from offensive French soldiers: *"Sì, cantero,"* she answers, and begins singing for the oppressors a song of thinly disguised patriotism and courage. Her sarcasm is subtle, and the song must grow imperceptibly toward the allegro. Her real message is clear when she exhorts, *"Mortali! il vostro fato è in vostra man . . ."* The conflict between her love and her country is a beloved theme of Verdi, and the Siciliana that opens the last act has to have more than a hint of that conflict, of oncoming tragedy, if it is to be more than a song. The ending is fast and awesome in this opera, and the Scala production had every scenic virtue desirable.

I was in very good voice, I had prepared well, and I was looking forward to the evening. Then as soon as I entered there was a demonstration from a small but very loud group shouting, *"Brava Callas."* I had no idea what they meant, but they kept it up; they called out, "Maria, Maria" while I sang and then shouted, *"Brava Callas"* again. It was ridiculous to be facing a debut role at a Scala opening night with a hostile audience who wanted not me but another diva who was no longer singing. There could be no way to please those people. It was the first time that I had ever had a problem like this, although it would not be the last; only once, however, did it ruin my performance, and that would be the worst night of my career. For now I went on singing. I met the challenge, and I sang my heart out. During my last aria I could see Maria Callas in the stage box, and at the curtain calls I was happy that she did not acknowledge the shouts of "Maria, Maria" that oozed through the applause, but that she gave me a standing ovation instead.

Still, I was furious; this was not the way to sing an opera, those people had come not to enjoy the music but to try to ruin it. Some even came backstage, behind the reporters who followed me to my dressing room. So when a gossip columnist asked me what I thought of what had happened, I made a mistake, I said, "Let them get Callas to come and do *Vespri,* if she can sing." I did not want to offend Callas, but I was angry, understandably so. So I made a mistake. The scandal sheet the next day wrote of the terrible fight between Scotto and Callas. Callas had nothing to do with the problem; she hadn't asked those people to come and ruin the evening; she was there to see the opera.

By the third performance the claque was wild and it was very difficult to sing; the management of La Scala did not seem to be able or willing to do anything about the disturbances, and the whole affair left a very bad taste in

my mouth; not for the opera, which I went on to sing
many times, but for La Scala and for these hysterical fans
whom I had been fortunate enough not to meet before but
who now seemed to be all over that theater.

La Scala asked me if I would sing in a new production
of Donizetti's *Linda di Chamounix* for the next season as
well as in Verdi's *Simon Boccanegra*. *Linda* I was very interested in, but I had seen *Simon Boccanegra* once and did not
think much of the soprano lead. Abbado wanted me for it.
The management insisted and two months later suggested
that we go to Naples to hear a production of *Simon* there,
to see if I would change my mind. I went to Naples, saw
the opera, still did not think much of it, but thought I
might as well agree.

We waited for the contract in Gonzaga. Already it
was summer and there was no contract for either *Linda* or
Simon. Lorenzo called and was told to come in and talk
with Luciano Chailly (artistic adviser of La Scala and the
young conductor's father) since Siciliani was away. There
he was told that I was to sing the *Linda* production only,
that someone else had been hired for the *Simon*. Lorenzo
called Abbado into the meeting and he confirmed that
Giorgio Strehler, the director, had insisted on Freni; they
had not dared to call and tell us directly but had let me go
ahead and prepare the role and just hope that I would be
relieved not to have to sing it since I had not wanted it
very much. I was not amused. And I never returned to La
Scala. It was not because of the *Vespri* problems with the
Callas claque. It was because of the lack of consideration
and professionalism on the part of the management.

As for the problem with fanatics, it is very sad. Imagine that you do your job every day, say you are a secretary

or a welder, and that you do it very well; but all you hear is that your predecessor did it better. You keep working and still you hear the same thing: you are not like your predecessor, your predecessor did a much better job. Eventually you will be very angry, not only at those who tell you these things but also at the predecessor too. You will say, "Why don't you get her to come and do the job if you want her so much?" That is all that happened in the Callas controversy, and that is all that happens when I get so angry at these people. I remember how Callas had to face hostile fans in the same theaters, and how she left La Scala in terrible disappointment. It is disillusioning and unfair. If it were not for my family it would hurt so much more, but *"Vissi d'arte"* is not my song. I have a life outside the theater, so my love for it is only one aspect of my love for life. And that I will never lose.

Nine

A Met Homecoming

In the fall of 1967 we returned to Milan from New York and found a terrible surprise awaiting us in our apartment at number 7 Piazza Diaz. Some of the furniture was gone, as were the silverware, jewelry, paintings, vases, money from the safe, and anything we thought of looking for: all the souvenirs of my career, a Viotti trophy, a Golden Olive Wreath, many other things. The robbers had taken everything.

Later we found out that the cleaning woman Clara was actually the leader of a gang of thieves operating out of Milan and stealing all over Switzerland and northern Italy. They were caught by the detectives of Interpol as I rehearsed *Lucia* for that Lullo-Abbado production. No one had been hurt in the incident, but it did have something to do with our deciding to move to the country and build a house for ourselves in Gonzaga, Lorenzo's hometown.

Gonzaga is a golden town that reached a peak of splendor in the fifteenth century but since then has neither grown very much nor deteriorated at all. It is a very well kept secret that Lorenzo's family came upon years ago. The beautiful countryside is never more than a few blocks away, and the center of town near the landmark of the old Piazza Castello is the eighteenth-century Piazza Matteotti with the Hotel Villa Gina at one end. To this piazza people from even smaller towns come every Wednesday and turn the square into a marketplace for the best vegetables and fruits, for the freshest mozzarella and for parmesano aged just right. To drink Italy's best Lambrusco we could turn to our own vineyards. It is not far from the rivers Mincio and Po, an easy drive from Mantua and Parma and even Verona.

Our house was designed by a good friend, the architect Armando Donnamaria, who is Paolo Washington's brother-in-law. There was no direct train from Milan. Lorenzo's parents would be near, the children could enjoy swimming and playing and being safe. We all felt very safe and very good.

Then in 1976 something happened that was even more unpleasant and frightening than the Milan robbery. Lorenzo and I were in Parma for the afternoon, working on *Luisa Miller*. I remember that it was the final dress rehearsal and of course I needed Lorenzo to see it. Meanwhile my mother was playing cards with Lorenzo's parents back in Gonzaga, as the children played with their baby-sitter before going to bed. Suddenly the door was thrown open and four masked men ran in; they beat up Lorenzo's father, tied everyone with rope, and locked the children in the closet. They took everything, and the children were terrified; we soon learned that our poor dog hadn't made a sound because the robbers had taken care to drug his food earlier. They were never caught.

At this point we had a house in New York as well, and we had to decide where the children would be safest and how to spend less time away from them. A friend pointed out that we had actually been very lucky that the children were so young and had only been tied up and scared; babies are a bother for kidnappers, but slightly older children are a gold mine. Now I was terrified. This had nothing to do with politics; I sing everywhere from New York to Moscow, Budapest to Buenos Aires, and I love my public and my art the same in every theater; this had to do with fear for the children—kidnappings were in the news in Italy then, more often than I cared to read.

So when the opportunity came we moved to the United States to stay. This would not have been possible if I had not been returning to the Metropolitan Opera. My last appearance at the Met under Bing had been a *Lucia* just after the birth of Filippo. It was not a very good performance: I remember that I had had a great loss of calcium during the pregnancy and my health was not in the best shape. It was the only time in my life that I caught cold constantly. The chance to return to the Met came after Bing had left.

At the end of August 1974 another soprano canceled her entire run of *I vespri siciliani* at the Met. I had just had several successes in that opera, and the Met needed me on extremely short notice to sing the role of Elena. At the time I was rehearsing *Madama Butterfly* in San Francisco for my debut in that city. I was interested in singing *Vespri* at the Met, however, so I tried to work something out. But Kurt Herbert Adler, the director of the San Francisco Opera, explained that my debut was eagerly anticipated in San Francisco and that he certainly could not come up with another *Butterfly* on short notice, so he refused to release me. Then the Met called back and asked if I would be available at any time for any performance of *Vespri* later in the season and said that they would wait to hear from me before hiring another soprano for the days when I could not sing.

So after I finished *Butterfly* in San Francisco I returned home to New York for my first rehearsal of *Vespri* at the Met. The Met's new artistic director, James Levine, was there; it was our first meeting. And the other principals were Plácido Domingo, Sherrill Milnes, and Paul

Plishka. Finer men could not be assembled in any cast, and I was very happy.

My relationship with Maestro Levine began that day and has grown ever since. The moment when a great conductor and a famous singer meet for the first time can be tense. It is an encounter that can turn magic or tragic. Jimmy and I looked in each other's eyes and I knew that tragedy was not in store; we became friends. I was excited to find him and he was just as excited to find me. One cannot underestimate professional joy because it is not found as often as people might think. With Jimmy it is sheer pleasure each time to discover music together, it is always a true collaboration. And it is not that we are close friends outside the theater, actually. I am very private, I dislike backstage politics, and I tend not to hang around the stage when I am not working; there are places in the Met or in any other theater where I still get lost! That is the beauty of my relationship with Maestro Levine, that together we are intimate friends of the music. He is a professional and so am I, and onstage we can become one friend in the service of music.

I feel particularly at home at the Metropolitan Opera, and there are twenty-five good reasons for this: twenty-five roles in my twenty years on that stage. In 1965–66 I began with Cio-Cio-San in Puccini's *Madama Butterfly* and followed that in the same season with Lucia in Donizetti's *Lucia di Lammermoor* and Adina in *L'elisir d'amore*. In 1966–67 I was Violetta in Verdi's *La Traviata* at the Met. In 1971–72 I was Gilda in Verdi's *Rigoletto* and Marguerite in Gounod's *Faust*. Amina in Bellini's *La Sonnambula* and Mimì in Puccini's *La Bohème* followed in 1972–73. In 1973–74, Elena in *Vespri*. In 1975–76, all in one night, Giorgetta, Suor Angelica, and Lauretta in Puccini's *Il Trittico*. In

1976–77, Leonora in Verdi's *Il Trovatore*, Berthe in Meyerbeer's *Le Prophète*, and Musetta in *La Bohème*. Cilèa's *Adriana Lecouvreur* in 1977–78. In 1978–79, Desdemona in Verdi's *Otello*, Luisa in Verdi's *Luisa Miller*, and Queen Elisabetta di Valois in Verdi's *Don Carlo*. In 1979–80, Ponchielli's *La Gioconda* and Puccini's *Manon Lescaut*. When a strike kept Puccini's *Tosca* out of the theater in 1980–81, I sang her with the Met in Central Park. I sang Bellini's *Norma* in 1981–82, and Verdi's Lady Macbeth in 1982–83. In 1983–84 there was Zandonai's beautiful *Francesca da Rimini*. And in 1984–85 it is with the Met that I return to Mozart for the first time in more than twenty years, as Vitellia in *La clemenza di Tito*. Yes, I have given much to this house, and it has given me much too.

After *I vespri siciliani* the Metropolitan Opera asked if I would be interested in doing one New Year's Eve *Butterfly* and then some *Butterflies* in the parks during the summer. The idea of staying in New York to work in the early summer accorded well with my children's plans, but I did not want to accept without at least mentioning that I did not want to repeat *Butterfly* every year. Anywhere else it might not have occurred to me, but you can see why I might worry at the Met. There was no problem. Even as we agreed on plans for the summer we were figuring out when else I would be free and what the plans for the future might be. I remember that Jimmy mentioned that they were thinking of doing Puccini's *Il Trittico* and he asked if I would like to do my first Suor Angelica or any other role in those three operas. Why not all three? I answered. And all three I did. I guess the "turn" that Bing had told me to wait for had finally arrived.

In 1975–76 I gave two complete *Tritticos* and then repeated the roles on tour. I also had a revival of *Butterfly* with the Met at Wolf Trap in Vienna, Virginia, that caused the Washington *Post* to call me "the finest singing actress today." The following season I had my first *Il Trovatore* at the Met, a new production of *La Bohème*, and a new production of *Le Prophète*. New productions, new roles, and telecasts followed in *Luisa Miller, Don Carlo, Manon Lescaut, Otello,* while my activity in this country increased as I wanted to stay closer to the family: I sang my first *Tosca* in Philadelphia and my first American *Norma* in Cincinnati. If I had been pigeonholed before, I was totally free now. It is like the decathlon champion who finds joy not in the laurel wreaths that crown him at the end of the race—he loves the race itself. The rewards may be generous, and so they are with music, but none is so satisfying as the song itself. To be able to share so often such great music and drama with an audience is to be very happy.

La Bohème at the Met was a particular pleasure, because it was the first live telecast of an opera and in one night we were going to reach more people than had seen Puccini's opera since its premiere. I remember that Filippo was almost in the production but backed out because he and Laura never like to see the last acts of operas—their mother usually dies at the end. The telecast was beautiful in every respect except one: I hated the way I looked.

To put it simply, I was fat. Looking at the videotapes gave me a new perspective on myself. And now that with television I was going to have such a large audience, I felt that audience did not deserve such a large singer. The experience apparently did not affect the tenor of that evening in the same way, but for my part I decided to lose weight. I wanted to be as effective as possible on television because I am convinced that it is the most important way to bring opera to the people in our time. With television, opera is not limited to the relatively few who can come to the theater, but a single performance is literally seen by millions; opera can never be for an elite again. Now, after years of study I knew I had to change one more time, that I had to change my appearance to help make opera look like a modern theatrical experience.

Dieting was not easy. I am Italian, after all. I love food, especially pasta, wine, lots of sleep, no exercise. Besides, I had known hunger, real hunger, in my youth. I don't think that anyone who has been truly poor ever forgets it, and food was a treasure that I would never take for granted, a reminder that things were better than before. Now my treasure was keeping me from being the singer I could be. So I went to a specialist in Modena who put me on a strict diet for one year. I lost thirty pounds and have kept my weight the same since. Some people worry that losing weight might hurt the voice and I say nonsense: that is a myth to protect the fat singers. My best years have been my forties, when I have been thin and fit. Now I take no long naps but swim and play tennis instead; I walk four times more than I used to; and every day I do barre exercises that a friend from the Bonn Opera ballet taught me while I was there singing.

The most important thing is the will power, and the hardest has been giving up pasta. I compensate by cooking it for my friends, especially on tour. But to be a good cook takes time, and most of my real cooking is done in Gonzaga when we are there for the summer; on tour I just invent quick recipes and try them. For frank advice I can rely on my friend Larry Stayer, and on Charlie Riecker. I have developed a new passion for porcelain and try to hunt for statuettes in antique shops wherever I happen to be singing. I basically hate sports, except for fishing when

I can just sit and wait for the fish. But on tour lately, whereas I used to rest between performances, I stay outdoors more. Sometimes my Met buddies Charles Anthony and James Morris will take me fishing. I can listen to the song of the fish and think of my uncle Salvatore. Other times I become a bit braver. I remember while in Atlanta with the Met we had a baseball game of Metropolitan Opera versus the Emory University coaches. The coaches did not need to fear for their laurels that day, but I did receive the honor of being named the Met's very short shortstop.

Ten

Puccini

After thirty years with *Madama Butterfly*, I have some very definite ideas on how to sing it, on how to approach the postromantic repertory and its greatest operatic exponent, Puccini. For the acting I credit the experience and good advice, and for the singing I credit bel canto, which means simply singing well and singing beautifully—good advice for any repertory. Verismo is a little more difficult because it is so much more realistic yet so concentrated; but the responsibility of the artist is the same: to give meaning, depth, and clarity to the words within the music.

Fashions come and go in all the arts, and every period finds new virtues and rediscovers and rescues the art of one or another time. In the case of painting or sculpture the matter is not complicated: when a work is seen in a new light all that is needed is to display it in that light. In music, the singer must recreate the work before a reappraisal is possible. She is no creator, but without her care, sensibility, and service the music may never be known. The responsibility is awesome.

Much verismo had a bad reputation as I was learning it, and I have felt compelled throughout my career to rediscover it and display it in a clean, bright light. The aim of such a task is not to recreate an exact replica of a musical work at the time of its premiere. This would be impossible since the meaning of music is not timeless; it lies in the performance to an audience and, no matter how meticulously we may reproduce the original musical conditions, we cannot reproduce the original audience. An authentic performance is found in the tension between the original musical sensibility and the demands of the time.

Not amazingly, the great composers provided for these contingencies in their scores. I confess that I draw from literary sources in no small amount when I am creating a character; I read the original novels or plays, the history of the period, the letters of the composer and librettist. But for ultimate answers I turn again and again to the score. In the score I begin and with the score I am satisfied.

Think of an example from early Verdi, such as Violetta's aria from *La Traviata*, Act I. *"È strano"* is a revelation in sung recitative, as for the first time Violetta wonders if after so many men perhaps this young admirer has something different to tell her; she feels something new, maybe love; maybe for the first time, love. The phrases here are cushioned by chords as the situation is explained and the aria begins: a melodic flight in cavatina form with spectacular music of Violetta's new possibilities; then another transition in andante, *"Follie,"* another situation explained in song: she likes who she is, it would be madness to change now; this leads to the cabaletta, *"Sempre libera,"* with vocal virtuosity becoming the expression of Violetta's desperate freedom. The scene takes about ten or more pages of music.

Now think of an aria from Puccini, like *Madama Butterfly*'s *"Un bel dì."* As we saw when we discussed the opera earlier, there are at least as many emotional and plot turns in this aria as there are in Violetta's scene. But it is all done in just two pages of music, with a more diverse and freer structure. The style is different in that there is less sheer vocal virtuosity, but for the rest it is not much different from bel canto when it is sung the right way. From the very opening of *"Un bel dì,"* as Cio-Cio-San says that Pinkerton will come back, what is needed in singing are intonation, legato, pianissimi, and expression. The aria may not be divided into recitative, andante, transition or cabaletta, but the technical equipment needed to sing it is exactly the same. To think otherwise is to do a disservice to one repertory or the other. Where real changes in technique occur is in some of the modern music, say Alban Berg and later. Berg's *Lulu*, for example, calls for a different specialized technique, new ear training, bizarre jumps; it is all truly difficult. I love *Lulu*, but I do not specialize in this repertory, and there it makes sense for me to say no.

I have dedicated my voice to the repertory from bel canto through the Italian verismo. It is not that this is particularly an Italian style, I don't think; canzonette like *"O sole mio"* require such a style. It is just the style of the music and the way the vocal cords are trained. Verdi can be thought of as either verismo or bel canto, because he has everything; *Falstaff* can be verismo, and so can *Otello*. But by this I mean that he should be sung with style and care and that his directions are to be respected. Sloppy sobbings and lazy vocal technique became associated with verismo as an aberration. I have always tried to sing Puccini as the great music that it is. Often the difference is in the style of acting, which may vary with the sensibility of each period in history.

Having gathered all this knowledge over the years, I now felt secure enough to go back to that score that I took with me to the Canossian convent, the story of the girl who got lost on her way to her own convent. To Puccini's *Manon Lescaut*. Earlier in my life the Massenet *Manon* had been chosen for me. Now I chose Puccini. I first sang it in Dallas on November 15, 1979. I then sang it at the Met a few months later in the first live international telecast of an opera from the Metropolitan Opera. Of my first *Manon*

Lescaut, the critic John Ardoin wrote the next day in the Dallas *Morning News:*

> Someone has to be lying to us—this couldn't possibly have been the first Manon Lescaut of her career. It was too rich in vocal and dramatic detail, too spontaneous in its effect, too intelligent in its realization. There is no contemporary reference for her amazing achievement because no soprano today had managed to combine in this role in such exacting balance both elegance and earthiness. Here is an exceedingly human Manon, one both frail and frivolous, eager and loving. She was destined to play this part and sing these phrases. . . . How can one not be grateful to be part of a time which boasts a Scotto?

Every woman wants to be Manon, at least at one moment in her life. Every woman wants to be free to love whomever she wants, whenever she wants, to do the reckless, forbidden, and the dangerous at least once. The Puccini and the Massenet are two sides of the same woman, with Puccini being more faithful to the Prévost novel, but passionate *all 'italiana;* and Massenet being more faithful to its French spirit. I always want to have both in my repertory, and I wish it were possible to play them in one evening. At the Met the Des Grieux was Plácido Domingo, and with us were Philip Creech, Pablo Elvira, Mario Bertolino, Isola Jones, Andrea Velis, Julien Robbins, John Carpenter, and Russell Christopher. Gian Carlo Menotti directed and Desmond Heeley designed it. The conductor was Maestro James Levine. It was one of my favorite evenings at the opera, and I have repeated the role many times since.

Puccini's Manon is a passionate woman from beginning to end; she may even be older than Massenet's. She does not know enough to recognize or at least to want true love when it presents itself; she is the fifth essence of femininity, a spoiled creature who wants and wants, and what she wants is everything that money can buy. But when she achieves this she is bored and tries to overcome the strangeness of her rich surroundings by making fun of all those who she imagines really belong there. She is a spoiled coquette, only for a moment. Then Des Grieux returns to her and she is once again all passion, her music in the duet tells us that. In Massenet, Manon dies in Le Havre, but with Puccini and Prévost she goes to Louisiana. In the book what happens is that the nephew of the governor tries to take advantage of Manon because he is sure that she is an easy woman, and when Des Grieux finds out he has a duel with this man. That is why they have to run away and why in the last act of Puccini's opera Des Grieux and Manon are alone in an arid, barren marsh. It is the eighteenth century, and there are not many cities in the American colonies; they wander and wander, and Manon dies of exhaustion. Manon's death is one of the most moving and most difficult scenes I sing. The tendency here as with all verismo is to give too much, which is never good. Manon is alone, lost, abandoned, then she realizes her hopeless condition as she sings it and cries out, *"Orror."* The word cannot be declaimed. Many think that it is effective to speak or shout it, but Puccini marked it pianissimo and Puccini knew Manon better than any singer. Here is this hungry, thirsty, hopelessly lost woman, her drama is realistically drawn in the music, and the horror must be almost whispered but always on the A in the score. The fortissimo should be *"non voglio morir,"* because even if Manon has no strength left at all, almost no life, she still always has one final rebellion to say, "No, I don't want to die, I don't want to die. When I sing this Manon I become that young and foolish girl, so full of love and pleasure, so lost; I completely lose myself in *Manon Lescaut.*

With Puccini's *Il Trittico,* I became the first soprano in Metropolitan Opera history to sing all three Puccini heroines—Giorgetta, Lauretta, and Suor Angelica—in one evening. I did it several times, and I know that I prefer this to perhaps singing only one or two of these roles separately. It is fantastic to become these three women in one night, to explore the three ways in which Puccini presents the theme of death in these operas. In *Il Tabarro,* Giorgetta's story shows us the violent death that comes with murder. The heroine of *Suor Angelica* is transfigured in an ecstasy of love and forgiveness as she dies by her own hand. And in *Gianni Schicchi,* Lauretta is the sweetest component of a joke about death, in which a corpse brings about her happiness.

Il Tabarro is a tale of frustration, and this tension should be obvious from the moment of Giorgetta's entrance into the riverboat; her body, her guarded moves, and the defiant tilt of her head should bespeak her despair. She has lost her child, and she has lost her love for her husband; she is trapped on this river with an older man she no longer loves, and she is desperate. When she meets Luigi he becomes more than just another man, he is her way out of all this, her salvation. Giorgetta is not a whore; her character is more complex than that. Her dreams are of small and good things, of things she does not have like love and a happy family, of freedom. Before the action of the opera begins, her child has died. When her husband murders Luigi, everything is lost. If her story were to continue, Giorgetta would probably commit suicide.

But instead Puccini takes us away from the tepid waters of the river to the pure and lovely air of the convent in *Suor Angelica*. But Angelica too is a woman who has lost everything. In a cold, aristocratic family, she grew up without affection and never had any until she met a man and made one mistake. The time is the seventeenth century, and she was made to pay dearly for having a child out of wedlock; she has been cloistered in a convent and the outside world is lost to her forever. Angelica's aunt brings her the horrible news that this child whom she never once held in her arms is now dead. She now has nothing, she wants to die, but she does not want to commit a mortal sin. She finally believes that in death she will be reborn and be united with her child, so she kills herself not consciously as a sin but as an act of hope. The incredibly beautiful *"Senza mamma"* finds the fragile nun imagining how it might have been with her child, that he might have had a mother, that she might have loved him. Only then does Angelica realize the enormity of her sin, and she begs forgiveness for her suicide. She is saved by a miracle, a miracle of salvation and liberation from sin. She dies seeing a vision of the child, an image that only she can see and the audience must believe. It is a beautiful role, a demanding character to play sensitively and completely.

Lauretta in *Gianni Schicchi* is a romp. She is a rich girl who is surrounded by a loving family, except that her father will not hear of her love for the young Rinuccio because he comes from a dreadful family. When Schicchi refuses to help her, she threatens suicide, but here it is a childish joke, she does not know what she is saying. When she sings, *"O mio babbino caro,"* she means her love for her father and for Rinuccio, and it is a very true and sweet moment.

I received more than ten thousand letters after my telecast of *Il Trittico* live from the Met, more than I have ever received in my life. So many were from people who had been moved by Angelica's devotion; many were from people who had not seen an opera before and thought that it was beautiful. And it is beautiful to sing and reach an audience in this new way.

The play *Tosca* was written by Sardou for Sarah Bernhardt, and from what I understand the Divine Sarah did everything that could be done on a stage and more when she became Tosca. When the play was made into an opera it remained easy to overdo; if verismo is always in danger of exaggerating the melodrama, the danger is nowhere as obvious as in *Tosca.* Here is a tale of a great diva, no less, with the added ingredients of political intrigue, torture, murder, sadism, attempted rape, and suicide. All in less than two hours. I decided to stay close to Puccini's score, where the action is indicated in great detail. And as I studied the score the character became clear. I decided to *sing* the role rather than shout lines that have traditionally been shouted. Only one line is indicated as *parlando* in Puccini's score, the outburst of *"Giuro."* Everything else has a specific pitch indication. Through the music I became Floria Tosca, the most recent of my Puccini characters.

Here I am a prima donna, a famous singer; I have a lover about whom I actually know very little, probably because I only want to hear about my life and don't care too much about his boring political activities. Suddenly I am caught in a revolution, I am taken from the Palazzo Farnese where I have been singing for the Queen and I am assaulted by the vile Scarpia: but more important, I am assaulted by real life for the first time. Tosca has been childish all her adult life, and now she is made to play with dangerous toys.

In Act II, after she is nearly raped by Scarpia, she becomes a woman. Her realization is in the form of an internal struggle against the brutality of life that she must now face. "I have lived for art, I have been so good, I have given my jewelry to the Church, why do I deserve all that is happening to me?" Even as she asks this, Tosca begins to realize how small these things are, how superficial her life has been, how real her tragedy has become. Soon she will hear drums that may mean her lover's death. This pathetic realization is at the heart of the famous *"Vissi d'arte,"* and only by singing that aria not as an aria but as a moment in Tosca's transformation into a woman can the dramatic integrity of the scene be maintained. It has been claimed by some that *"Vissi d'arte"* stops the action needlessly, that it does not belong in the opera. I think Puccini knew exactly what he was up to, and that was a lot more than giving the soprano a big aria. Let the musically nouveau riche show off technique and long notes and histrionics here; the way to sing *"Vissi d'arte"* is to follow the dramatic thread after the word ". . . *così.*" And then when Tosca must kill it will be understood as not playacting but real life, the first act of real life that this woman has been forced to perform.

Every singer, with or without reason, has felt the temptation to "live for art" as Floria Tosca has done in Puccini's opera. Beware Tosca's fate, it was not good. I think that if I had to pick an aria to live by it would not be

"Vissi d'arte" but rather *"Io son l'umile ancella"* from Cilèa's *Adriana Lecouvreur*. Adriana, as famous an actress as Tosca is a singer, tells her friends that she is the humble maiden of the creative spirit, that she has taken to her heart the gifts she has been given; she is the tone of the poem, the echo of human tragedy. She aspires only to truth. She is indeed only the servant of art, and of course every servant has a life outside her service. Adriana Lecouvreur was a woman while Floria Tosca was still a child.

I have sung every Puccini opera except *La Rondine* and *La fanciulla del West*. I would like to do both someday, and I am very interested in *Fanciulla*. My children would like me to do it because I would get to live at the end, and I think the role would be very good for me. In *Turandot* the real Puccini heroine is Liù, which I have sung and recorded; I am not crazy about the title role, and we will never know what Puccini might have done with it: at the moment when she should be dramatically alive, when she falls in love with Calaf, Puccini put down his pen forever. Liù is his last completed heroine.

Musetta I sang out of curiosity, not to get to know Musetta, but to see her friend Mimi from a new angle; she is all fun, but also she is a true friend to Mimi, and I will sing Mimi better for having understood Musetta. As for this less tragic bohemian, her most important moments are listening, not singing; and it is these, especially in Act IV, that I prepared especially carefully.

By preparing I mean literally preparing what to say. So many singers have all the notes ready but they come onstage and they have no idea what they are saying; they know what to sing but not what to say. The words free the music, they make it actually easier to sing. Learning this about acting in music is the gift from my directors for which I am most grateful. Concentration means being fully conscious of what the character is saying; without it, the singing is mechanical, or just plain bad. To make lovely sounds is not enough.

Eleven

Words and Music

Words shape everything. The voice must be secure, of course; and the technique must be clean. But when I am onstage I take for granted the vocal equipment through concentration. Then it is the words that shape the voice and color its sound. Every word counts in a great opera.

One of the most difficult passages in *Norma* is her last recitative, *"Ei tornerà,"* which reaches a high C within the recitative as that simple phrase reveals the only moment in the entire opera that Norma is happy. She has found a true friend in Adalgisa, a friend who will bring her lover Pollione back to her. Norma is secure for once, she is smiling and the smile is in the voice; when she says, "He will return," she knows that it will be as it was before, that he will love her as he did before. It is a moment of sweet nostalgic memory, and all of that intensity and passion must be clear in that simple recitative as it reaches a totally exposed, pianissimo high C. It must be a happy sound, Norma's only one in the whole score. And it must be well prepared. Working with great stage directors has been an integral part of my growth as an opera singer. I owe a great deal to John Dexter, Mauro Bolognini, Renato Castellani, Giorgio de Lullo, Peter Hall, Gian Carlo Menotti, Piero Faggioni, and Raf Vallone.

Bolognini and Castellani were both film directors first, and they helped me very much when I began the important part of my career. I have already mentioned how Castellani tied my hands at rehearsal when I moved them too much as Bellini's Juliet. "One gesture should explain the evening," he told me, and it is a lesson I did not forget. With Bolognini I worked on my first *Straniera* in Palermo in 1969; and on *La Traviata* at the Arena in Verona in 1970. *Traviata* of course was not new to me but I remember I thought Bolognini's concept fascinating—that the whole libretto was one long dramatic monologue in Violetta's mind. *La Straniera* was a turning point in my acting. When I knew the music inside out, Bolognini made me talk about the character in the simplest, clearest, and most profound terms, and we used these talks to work out a few simple, specific movements for this exotic Bellini heroine. A king has fled his wedding bed and has fallen in love with another woman, Agnese, to whom he has sent his portrait and a lock of his hair. She falls in love with the King and marries him, not knowing that he already has a wife. The Church threatens to excommunicate the King if he does not return home, so he leaves Agnese in a castle in Britanny where she will be watched. The poor girl manages to escape and live in solitude under the name Alaide. She becomes a mysterious stranger, and her character and her music are veiled by her fears. Working with Bolognini on *La Straniera*, I polished what I had been achieving since the first *Sonnambula* through the progress I had made in Castellani's *Capuleti e i Montecchi* and De Lullo's *Lucia di Lammermoor*. *La Straniera* was the road to *Norma*, and Bolognini was a great teacher along that road.

With John Dexter I worked for the first time on Meyerbeer's *Le Prophète*. I liked him instantly. He is a difficult man to know; he talks very little because he understands just when words are not necessary. And his directions are always very specific and very useful. I remember when we began working on the new production of *Don Carlo*, which was my first Elisabetta di Valois. I had been many things in my life that I could recall when creating a character: a wife, lover, mother, friend, poor and rich, fat and thin. But I had never been a queen! The character of Elisabetta was difficult at first, and John Dexter gave me concrete suggestions around which I began building my Elisabetta.

"Think, Renata, you are a queen, you must behave like a queen; notice how everyone is always looking at you but you never, never look at any of your subjects directly." I understood this, and the position of my head, my bearing, even my voice eventually took shape from that direction.

John is also the man who taught me how to sit while wearing those huge petticoats. "Try it this way," he suggested onstage, sitting on the very edge of a bench with the very edge of his seat, "and never let your body touch any other part of the chair." It worked.

John is a very practical man of the theater. I remember how he brought a brown horse to rehearsal to use as the Queen's horse.

"But, John, why a brown horse? A white one would be so much more beautiful, impressive."

"If I give you a white horse, everyone will look at the horse!"

"Oh." I swallowed. "Thank you, John."

I took many directions from John Dexter in the course of discovering the character of Elisabetta di Valois, a woman who can so easily be lost in the immense panorama that is the opera *Don Carlo*. Verdi's Elisabetta does not, perhaps cannot, look people in the eye. She sees all the reactions of the ruled, but after the Fontainebleau scene her gaze is never met by that of an equal. Her royal restraint is a chain. She allows herself to be a woman only when actually alone yet addressing someone of her own station in the devastating scene, *"Tu che le vanità."* Then torrents of passion overflow in her music.

There are difficult times, say with a new role or a particularly demanding passage in a new production, when it is difficult to relax and maintain confidence in oneself. I remember how John Dexter gave me some very good advice during one of these times. "Renata," he told me, "if you're nervous, just keep this thought in mind: you are onstage, you can look everyone in the eye and think, 'You come here and do it!' " The thought is a little unfair to the audience; after all, there may well be an engineer sitting out there who could tell me to come design his buildings, or a doctor daring me to cure his patients. Singing and acting are my job, not posing dares to the audience. But I have to confess that in moments in *Don Carlo* and *Macbeth*, John's suggestions were very comforting. As always, John Dexter gave me strong advice that helped me very much.

I worked with the director Piero Faggioni in 1984 in the new production of Zandonai's *Francesca da Rimini* at the Met, with Plácido Domingo as Francesca's lover Paolo and a fabulous cast that included Brian Schexnayder, Gail Robinson, Natalia Rom, Gail Dubinbaum, Claudia Catania, Isola Jones, Richard Fredricks, Anthony Laciura, Nicole Lorange, John Darrenkamp, John Gilmore, John Bills; and, as Paolo's brothers, Cornell MacNeil and William Lewis. Maestro Levine conducted the opening night on March 9, 1984. The beautiful costumes were by Franca Squarciapino, the sets were by Ezio Frigerio; along with Faggioni, the two Italians were making their Metropolitan Opera debut. I put a lot of myself into creating the character of Francesca, and I was very happy with the results at the Met. *Francesca da Rimini* is a difficult work; it demands a strong cast, sensitive direction, and spectacular sets and costumes. The Act II battle alone must strain the resources of even the best theaters. The Metropolitan Opera mounted *Francesca* very well.

Piero Faggioni is an actor as well as a director, and the role of d'Annunzio's Paolo is one that he has played on stage; he knew the play inside out, and this helped me immensely. For my part I began by studying the play even before coming to the score, but I found the transition easy because the words of d'Annunzio remained in the libretto, and Zandonai's music reflects these words perfectly. I have worked with many librettos, and I have to say that *Francesca da Rimini* is one of the best, that I have ever read. And Faggioni gave me everything possible to give to the character of Francesca, one of my best-thought-out characters.

Not far into his *Inferno,* Dante encountered the sad Francesca in the place where sinners of the flesh are punished. In Canto V, lines 121–23, the poet has questioned her and she replies:

> *Ed ella a me: "Nessun maggior dolore,*
> *che ricordarsi del tempo felice*
> *nella miseria; e ciò sa il tuo dottore."*

"There is no greater pain," she tells him, "than to recall happy times in sorrow; and this your teacher knows." This passage is the most popular in Dante, and has given birth to thirty operas. The play of Gabriele d'Annunzio transformed the tale while remaining close to the melancholy of Dante's Francesca. Zandonai's opera inhabits a world beyond verismo, faithful to the mystery of the play, almost ineffably beautiful. He has been called an Italian Debussy, or an Italian Strauss; and these labels bother me. He is an Italian composer, and he should be better known. The character of the tragic adulteress Francesca is fascinating. She is a woman of her time, religious and resigned to an unhappy marriage for the sake of her family. But she loves another and has loved him from the beginning; her passion is searing and her fall inevitable. In the second act she finally begs Paolo to give her peace, in the hope not of a life together but only an hour of sweet oblivion, a moment of escape from the tempest of her wretched life. *"Paolo, datemi pace!"* she bursts, giving herself up totally to her doom. The peace she begs from Paolo is simply peace of mind; she does not want to betray her husband. Yet it was Paolo whom she thought she had married, and her marriage to Gianciotto had been but a cruel trick: she would never have married him knowingly. When the inevitable adultery occurs, Gianciotto murders both Paolo and Francesca.

Because it is so little known now, we were very careful to create *Francesca da Rimini* in the correct style, for the fragrance of Zandonai's world is very much his own. Here as in every opera, style is an achievement as well as a necessity. The role of Francesca is physically very demanding because her body must tell so much even when she is not singing.

With Puccini's *Manon Lescaut* I became a more physical actress, jumping on the beds, making love on the floor. I had to pay attention to the smallest detail of what kind of material makes for the best hoop skirt when you are planning to roll around the floor. I worked on *Manon Lescaut* with a man whom I had last encountered in Cairo, in the score of *Amelia al ballo*.

Gian Carlo Menotti is not only a great director but of course a great composer as well, and his understanding of the stage is complete. He knows just what singers can and cannot do, although he can be amazed sometimes at just how much the vocal demands can be adjusted to the stage action. He directed my *Manon Lescaut* at the Met, and it is my favorite Puccini production.

Peter Hall was a revelation. Working on Lady Macbeth with him was a true collaboration of a very satisfying kind. Like Menotti, he can sometimes be surprised by how much a singer can do. He would ask, "Are you sure you can sing if I make you roll around the floor?" or "Can you hit the B-flat while bending over to pick up that candle?" I would ask him just to explain whatever he wanted me to do and I would do it; I trusted his sense of the stage. We discussed how the Sleepwalking Scene required other clothes than I had been given, a grimy gown creaking with layers of drippings of wax; that I should be barefoot and have my hair in a mess. It is not a moment for glamor. He agreed to this and other costume changes; and although this was not my first Lady Macbeth, I refined my character with him.

Verdi's tale is about two splendid monsters, not so much larger than life as larger than death. I first sang the opera at Covent Garden in a new production directed by Elijah Moshinsky and conducted by Riccardo Muti. We all worked hard and musical matters went very well from the beginning, but the stage directions were not very specific and we were left very much on our own to find the difficult characters of Macbeth and Lady Macbeth. Peter Hall at the Met was very good for me. He does not give so many specific directions, and things like the Sleepwalking Scene were improvised in rehearsals. But he knew Shakespeare's Lady Macbeth very well, and through her I came to know Verdi's. Here is a woman with perverse ambition but even more perverse, enormous and visceral love. And it is because she loves Macbeth that the futility of having made him King drives her to madness. Not at all like my only other somnambulist onstage, Lady Macbeth is almost dead as she walks in the last act; she is a shadow of past terror, now barely remembered. With Peter Hall I learned a great lesson: that that woman's monstrous cruelty, her ugliness, should never freeze the humanity out of the music.

I was very surprised that Peter Hall's *Macbeth* drew so much critical venom. If a capricious director were to ask me to do something outrageous for the sake of shock and contrary to what the composer intended, I would say no immediately; but that was not the case with Sir Peter. His romantic production made good dramatic sense. I remember once in Florence, when I was to sing Desdemona right after that beautiful first *Otello* at the Met, that the Hungarian director had several ideas on how to improve on Verdi. Desdemona, he told me, would have an alter ego who would haunt her during the love duet. I was not too sure what he meant but I didn't pay much attention until the final dress rehearsal, when the alter ego really became obvious: as Otello sang *"Venere splende . . . ,"* the stars didn't appear, but this woman wearing my wig but nothing else came up onstage behind me. I screamed. I was embarrassed, the poor nude dancer was embarrassed, we all had an attack of the giggles and Riccardo Muti decided that we should give *Otello* in concert form.

Another time, some years ago in Bonn, I sang a

Norma in Spanish Civil War costume, with *"Casta diva"* sung from the hood of a truck. It worked too, but it takes an audience less conservative than New York's for a production like that to work.

Raf Vallone was my choice to direct my first *Norma* in Turin's Teatro Regio in 1974, and then we worked twice on *Adriana Lecouvreur.* We had never met before *Norma* and he had never directed an opera before; but I had seen his work as an actor and director onstage and in films and I knew that he would be perfect, so I asked him. He turned to opera from the dramatic stage much as one might dream of returning to childhood, to the poetic curiosity we all once knew. We explored *Norma* together. There is never anything superfluous about his direction. He made an asset out of the limits of the music, something not all dramatic stage directors learn to do, and he worked with me always within the music to achieve simple gestures. For *Adriana* we worked on the text together and realized how much truth there was for a singer in the aria *"Io son l'umile ancella,"* that is all we are. The humility of that song began the first layer of Adriana's character, a fascinating woman who must not be allowed to overact her impulses on stage. By this time we were old friends, and Raf told a reporter, "The wonderful thing about Renata is that she comes to you every time as a virgin—she has no preconceived ideas. Her flexibility, her memory for gesture that is the expression of feeling, they are extraordinary." Of course I do often have preconceived ideas about a role, but I prefer to wait, to listen to the director and learn. Actually I am that flexible only with a great director, and it is his sensitivity that makes us both be so flexible in rehearsal. For *Norma* I had envisioned a classical style of acting, and that was what I received from Raf. He interviewed me before accepting the offer; he had never done opera before and he had never met me. I am glad that he accepted.

There are actors who always remain themselves, their personalities are strong and the role is secondary; it can be a wonderful experience in theater and opera, and many great performers always remain themselves while portraying a character. Then there are actors who *become* each character. Raf Vallone is one of these, and it was this quality that I wanted to achieve in my *Norma.* He knew nothing about the music, but he found out everything about the libretto, and that was fine. I do not need a director to help me with my singing; that, I know. It is the acting for which we all require help. That is why so many great directors are not musicians but men of the stage who respect music.

For *Norma* certain phrases seemed to be the keys to this woman's character, and only after mastering these did the rest of the role begin to fall into place. I did not change in very much on the way to the Met. In Florence I sang it in a production by Luca Ronconi, conducted by Riccardo Muti, that improved on the Turin *Norma* by having a soprano Adalgisa in Margherita Rinaldi. At the Met, with Fabrizio Melano directing and James Levine conducting, we had Tatiana Troyanos, Plácido Domingo, and Bonaldo Giaiotti. Should *"Casta diva"* be in G or F? Bellini wrote it in G, but he changed it to the key of F on the opening night, and these should be regarded as his final thoughts on the matter. It is not a consideration of tessitura, because he left the rest of the role as high as he first wrote it; it is a matter of feeling. I don't know why, but every soprano's best note is the B-flat, and it is there that singing the aria in F takes you; it's appropriate for the soft mood of prayer on a moonlit night. With the higher key the B natural is harsher and the scene can become a coloratura showpiece. *"Casta diva"* is not an aria meant to show off vocal effects. The rest of the role is very much up, the feeling always very musical. When I am asked what I want for my *Norma* I always reply, "An Adalgisa who can sing in the right key." This means two sopranos, or a very high mezzo like Troyanos or Agnes Baltsa in the duets. Troyanos is the finest Adalgisa singing today. At the Met no one seemed to notice what an achievement it was for her that we sang the entire score in the original keys. It was one of the rare times in the Met's history that the Norma-Adalgisa duets had been given that luxury.

Along with the great conductors are the coaches who can be a singer's best friends. They work on the musical side of the role and help in vocal matters as the preparations progress. The role of James Levine of course need not be mentioned: every great maestro is a great coach. My husband Lorenzo has always been my coach since the day of our wedding, and it is he who first hears my thoughts, musical or otherwise, on every role; I trust him completely. David Stivender is one of my best friends, and he finds music for me; he is a gifted musicologist—it was he who found the pages from Verdi's "Album" that I was honored to premiere in Washington and New York. Thomas Fulton is a fine conductor and pianist but, more important, he is a good friend to me. He has been my conductor and accompanist onstage and on records, working with me all year long on my recital programs and helping me choose my music. He coached me for my first *Norma* in New York, and he helped me to regain my confidence afterward. Why my confidence needed rebuilding is all part of another, sadder story.

To tell you about another very good friend I have to go back to 1965, the year of my Met debut. Three young men became special fans: Jeff Ruggiero, and Bob. They would all come to my dressing room or my hotel to talk about my performances. One of them joined the army and another left town, so we wrote letters but eventually lost touch with each other. Bob Lombardo stayed in New York after law school and we became very close. I was most impressed with his advice and relied on his friendship. One day I remember asking him, "Why don't you consider becoming an artists' manager, Bob? I think you would be very good." I had been through Columbia Artists, Sol Hurok, and one other firm; I knew what I was talking about. "You can start with me," I told him. So I became the first client of Robert Lombardo Associates, and Bob is still my manager. Except that it is not fair to describe him as my manager because he is more than a manager. He is my friend.

Making recordings can be a harrowing experience, and making record deals is worse. When I began recording for CBS Masterworks I was fortunate to have two friends who took care of me in artistic and personal matters and were always very considerate. One was Ernest Gilbert, who introduced me to CBS and is still a good friend. And the other was the late Marvin Saines, to whom I dedicated my recording of Respighi's *Il Tramonto*.

Who else is a friend? Acoustics. The best and friendliest acoustics for a singer are always in those houses built in the nineteenth century, when the orchestra was kept partly under the stage where it belongs. There is no improving on those perfect old horseshoes, and many modern theaters create a sound more like a symphonic concert with voices than opera. My favorite-sounding theaters have been the San Carlo in Naples, the Teatro Colón in Buenos Aires, the Paris Opéra, La Fenice in Venice, and the Bolshoi in Moscow. La Scala has strange acoustics, the result of restoration following the bombings in World War II. Of the newer theaters, I really love the new Metropolitan Opera, the Vienna Staatsoper, Covent Garden, and the Kennedy Center Opera House in Washington, D.C. Tokyo also has a great opera house, and I am told that the Sydney Opera House is a theater I would like; I have never been to Australia, and I hope that I can sing there someday.

The Verona Arena is exceptional acoustically. Its sound is a mystery to modern scientists and as magical to audiences today as it must have been through the centuries. I remember when I sang *La Bohème* in Verona and I was concerned that Mimi's last lines be audible; after all, this is an outdoor amphitheater with natural sound for thirty thousand people. So Lorenzo went during the dress rehearsal and sat in the very last row as far from the stage as possible. He came back and told me that he could hear Mimi's every whisper as if I had been sitting next to him. Rome's Baths of Caracalla are a different matter. The place was not meant to be a theater and it doesn't sound like one. It is windy and uncomfortable; I sang there only once, *Rigoletto*, and the scenery flew onto my head during the storm scene. I have not returned.

Singing outdoors always has its own surprises, of course. I remember the thrill of singing for an audience of two hundred thousand in Central Park in New York City when the Met produced *Tosca* there one summer. Ravinia is fabulous, as was the old Wolf Trap Farm. It is a typically

American kind of theater that has not caught on else-where: half covered, half open, with natural acoustics in-side and microphones for the open section. It works very well.

And what about the audiences who listen in these acoustical environments we call theaters? They vary from country to country in small ways—how they ask for auto-graphs, how they wait at the stage door. But by and large they are as universal as the music, the same everywhere from Moscow to New York, from Buenos Aires to Lon-don. A good performance invites a good reception, and a bad performance does not. Fans help, of course; and fanat-ics do not. I have been fortunate to have many good fans; most just write letters, which I love to answer. Some send presents that vary from flowers and jewelry to more ex-travagant things. A fan in Buenos Aires one season made sure that I had a different Rolls-Royce waiting at the stage door each night; another time, in New York, I received a series of tapes from a fan singing along with me on one of my records. After the television broadcast of *Il Trittico* live from Lincoln Center I received more than ten thousand letters; from that batch one stands out, from a dear fan called Sara. A religious woman, she had been ill for some time following personal problems. She wrote me many sad letters saying how only music kept her afloat but how lately even that was not helping and she was growing sad-der and sadder. Before the broadcast I wrote to her and told her the story of *Suor Angelica*, and I told her to watch the television but to imagine herself in a church and to pray along with Suor Angelica to Puccini's music. She wrote me a few days later that she had been cured, that she was no longer depressed. She is fine now, cured by Suor Angelica; she writes me five letters a day.

There are of course fanatics as well, the unpleasant kind, violent vermin who are as destructive to music as they are to religion or politics. Fanaticism destroys. A few years ago I had a particularly bad experience when posters of me in advertisements for public radio were defaced around Lincoln Center. Worse yet, I was physically attacked by a wild-haired young man who was perhaps a fan of some tenor, right on Broadway and Sixty-sixth Street. But overall I have been lucky that such fanaticism, for or against me, has not been typical of my career.

I have been lucky, too, in musical matters to have many fine colleagues. And for a colleague, if I must choose, I will take one with dramatic intentions similar to mine over one with similar vocal qualities. Take Mario Sereni, a great singing actor and one of my oldest and best friends. What a joy it is to sing with him, or just to talk, play cards, reminisce about friends we miss like the great Robert Merrill. Take Tatiana Troyanos. We have been told that our voices do not blend well, and in a strictly musical sense that is true: we have different timbres and vibratos, and our textures in duets are far from being alike. This is no great evil; we have the same approach to music and the drama, and our intentions make the music work when we sing together.

Of course there are also times when the blend is ideal. To be onstage with Plácido Domingo is always to celebrate music, to collaborate in the act of creation. Offstage he is his own man and as private as I am; I don't think I know him well. But onstage we are never Scotto and Domingo, we are Desdemona and Otello, or Manon and Des Grieux. I think I love Plácido so much because, although he is a real star, he behaves not like a star but like an artist. Alfredo Kraus is also a great artist and an old friend; onstage he always does his best to please the composer and through that to please the audience.

Then there is the great Jon Vickers. I remember while we rehearsed for the televised opening-night *Otello*, I thought what a difficult man this was. Jon demands great concentration at work, and he is very possessive about his interpretation of a role. He insisted on the particular way in which I should move as Desdemona—for example, telling me just how long to stay on the floor after he threw me down in our confrontation, he tried to block how I should weep in the mud and told me to stay down. I had some ideas about Desdemona, and after all I was the one playing her. We argued, we understood each other—and we made two fine characterizations together. Toscanini used to refer to the subhuman *testa di tenore* jokingly, but his jest could never have applied to men like Vickers, Kraus, and Domingo. They don't have the heads of tenors but of artists.

I remember in the last scene of *Otello* with Jon, who is such a powerful man, how he came at me. He grabbed my wrist and threw me down on the bed with all his might—and in Franco Zeffirelli's production at the Met that bed is not soft. My knee was swollen and bandaged for days. But I never told Jon, because he might then be afraid to hurt me and the scene worked so well. And each night when he grabbed my throat, Desdemona's terror was not entirely Scotto's acting: I was afraid for my life.

Giacomo Aragall and José Carreras are also among the great tenors; both are a pleasure to sing with, particularly in the way of purely musical joys since both of these men have such ravishing instruments that sometimes they can be tempted to choose vocal over dramatic virtues. I have sung often with the young American tenor Neil Shicoff, and I expect great things from him in the future.

Is a mezzo always a frustrated soprano? Only if she has what we can call the prima donna complex. Take my old friend Fiorenza Cossotto, for instance, who has been everything from my older brother in *Hansel and Gretel* to my nasty rival in *Adriana Lecouvreur*. Cossotto is a great mezzo-soprano, with a true low range that does not have to sink into chest tones. But she suffers from the prima donna complex, goes off to give Lady Macbeth a try, and returns to misbehave back home in mezzo roles. I remember an *Adriana Lecouvreur* at the Met, with Cossotto as the Princesse de Bouillon and José Carreras as Maurizio; during the *Phèdre* scene when, dramatically and musically, attention ought to be focused on Adriana's recitation, Cossotto picked a crucial moment to drop her fan loudly and then proceeded to invent a new stage business of telling the tenor to pick it up. It was small, but it did ruin a good scene. Giulietta Simionato never had a prima donna complex, and when she and Callas sang together there was never a question of Simionato's being seconda donna to Callas: there were *two* prime donne on those occasions. Tatiana Troyanos too is a great mezzo who has no need to acquire the prima donna complex. She is an artist. Marilyn Horne, of course, possesses not only a beautiful instrument but also has a virtuosity that astounds.

I admire the same virtuosity in Joan Sutherland, a true soprano phenomenon. And while we are on the subject of sopranos, I will say that my deepest admiration among my generation is for Birgit Nilsson. What an instrument! To have trained a voice like hers to do what it does and to maintain such enormous vocal power for such a long time in the repertory she has chosen are phenomenal. We are all phenomenal in a sense, like high-wire art-ists or ballet dancers. We singers are not akin to the acro-bats or the actors, for what they do is physically normal. Singing is an unnatural act. We, like dancers, train our bodies to do the unnatural and in doing so we try to bring about uncommon beauty. So history will remember very well Birgit Nilsson, for her unparalleled vocal power; Joan Sutherland and Marilyn Horne for their ravishing virtuosity; and perhaps Renata Scotto, for revealing the drama of opera within the tension of words and music.

Twelve

Sediziose Voci*

---

* *Seditious Voices.*

When I was in San Francisco singing *Adriana Lecouvreur*, with Aragall as Maurizio, I began talking with the company about doing Donizetti's *Anna Bolena* for the opening of the 1979 season. It was an opera that I had sung and liked very much, and I was most interested in singing it in San Francisco. Kurt Herbert Adler, the company's director, agreed that it was a fine idea but said that first he must solve the problem of where to find a suitable production already in existence since that was all that the budget would allow. So it was agreed that I would sing on opening night in an unspecified opera. In the meantime, unbeknownst to me, a certain tenor was also offered the opening night by Adler, with the opera as yet unspecified again.

A long time ago I had known this man and worked with him. We had been friends, but as he and his career grew in every sense he began to be less a colleague and more an adversary of his first Italian friends. It did not affect me very much, because I had other real colleagues to work with; but I thought it was a pity. We were still cordial, and I remember many a good poker game with him and other friends like Mario Sereni, Claudio Abbado, and John Alexander backstage during the preparations for the first "live from the Met" telecast of *La Bohème* in 1976.

It was to be an important broadcast, of course. The premiere was on my birthday, and there was cake in my dressing room and reporters around. My Rodolfo would not accept any of Mimi's cake and did not even come by to wish me a happy birthday, which hurt me a bit. In the intermissions we each had an interview on television, and this was especially exciting because it was after all the very first telecast of an opera live from the Met. We were all hoping for success because we knew how much it would benefit our company and opera in general in this country where the arts have such a fragile financial life. So in my interview I took the chance of having the cameras live in front of me to speak directly to President Jimmy Carter and ask him please to give more federal money to the arts. I am an American resident now, and I thought it my duty to do this.

I tell all this in the way of a prelude, because that evening's Rodolfo now was to play Enzo in the opera *La Gioconda* by Ponchielli; and it was that opera that Kurt Herbert Adler decided to do for his opening night. San Francisco was sure that I would turn down this chance, since it was *Anna Bolena* that we had discussed when I was engaged for the opening. The idea excited me, however; it was after all a new role, in the late romantic period of Italian opera that I love so much; it was a leading role that demands everything from the voice, with its mixture of Verdian lines and raw veristic impulse, bel canto carried into the future. In other words, I said yes, to everyone's surprise.

Everything went smoothly until it was announced that this would be no mere opening night but the first international telecast, broadcast all over the world live from the San Francisco Opera stage. At that point my agent Robert Lombardo insisted on some fairly standard guarantees in my contract. First, my name would appear first, since I was the protagonist; in an opera like *Gioconda* such a clause is standard. Also, there would be photographs either alone or with all of my colleagues, since there was no valid dramatic reason for Enzo and La Gioconda ever to embrace as characters. The San Francisco Opera did not live up to either of these agreements.

That summer RCA records had planned sessions for a complete recording of *La Gioconda* with Jimmy Levine conducting, Plácido Domingo, and Tatiana Troyanos. Unfortunately an orchestra strike in Great Britain pushed the recording schedule beyond the RCA budget, and the project was canceled. Instead I recorded *Norma* and *Bohème* that summer, both with Levine conducting. The schedule was tight, but I wanted to live up to my agreement to be in San Francisco for rehearsals; so I checked and double-checked that San Francisco would have all the principals assembled, as promised in all of our contracts, for the beginning of these rehearsals. I did not spend any extra time in London and we worked very hard to finish that recording on time. I arrived in San Francisco only to be told that there was no tenor. We rehearsed without him, leaving a large hole in the blocking and not all the time I wanted to prepare this role, which was new for both of us. In rehearsals I like it to be as close as possible to the stage performance. I sing in full voice so that my vocal technique is secure enough to be taken for granted by the opening; I need to have my colleagues do the same.

Finally our Enzo arrived, but he canceled his first rehearsal with me without explanation. Then I received a phone call summoning me to his hotel room for a special rehearsal. "Are you sick?" I asked him, ready to help, but he was not sick. The reason that he had canceled rehearsal and now wanted it done in the privacy of his hotel room with just me and the maestro was that he had shown up at rehearsal not only days late but also not knowing the music! I had been recording two operas in the summer, but I managed to learn the score and show up at rehearsal ready and on time. The least this man could have done was to swallow his pride and come with score in hand to sight-read at rehearsal, but it is a little-known fact that he can't read music very well, and he needs someone to play the lines for him to then memorize. So this special rehearsal in his room was to save him embarrassment and to make me work so that he might get by on someone else's sweat.

I was reminded of the first time that I had encountered this man's musical irresponsibilities, and I had to laugh. It was 1969, in Rome, when we were preparing Verdi's *I Lombardi*. We were at a musical rehearsal with Maestro Gavazzeni and we worked on Giselda's beautiful aria with cabaletta when, in a vision, her dead lover sings to her in a beautiful tenor arioso before the cabaletta continues.

"What is this music? I am supposed to be dead."

"It's your aria," Gavazzeni replied patiently.

By now the entire Rome Opera cast and chorus was in tears of laughter; I think they may have thought he was kidding. He was not.

"But, really, I am supposed to be dead. No one told me. I don't know this music."

He had not tried reading the score, the surest way I have found to know not only my own part but perhaps to discover what the opera is about. It is appalling for a singer of any stature to pretend to be preparing a role in an opera without having the common sense to read the entire piece through to the end. That same person, larger but somehow unchanged by the years, was at it again.

I disliked rehearsing with him without his knowing the music, and I certainly would not rehearse in his hotel room. The next day he finally showed up and sang *"Cielo e mar,"* which he knew; then we began the encounter of

Enzo and Gioconda, and sure enough he made a musical mistake every other line, at which time we had to stop and let the pianist play the right notes for the tenor. This was ten days before the final dress rehearsal, but he was not worried because he would manage to get extra coaching and more of those special rehearsals. In the meantime, this was my first *Gioconda* too, and I was alone.

The San Francisco Opera expected me to quit and had hired Grace Bumbry to be standing by when I did. But I liked Ponchielli's opera, I had read all of it, I had learned it, and I was going to sing it. The premiere came and the reviews were very good. A television documentary crew was backstage from then until the telecast a few days later.

The television broadcast itself of course had to be rehearsed, particularly for the exigencies of this first satellite transmission live from the San Francisco Opera to Europe. A *terzetto*, a short trio, proved too long for television, and the director decided to cut it. I thought this might be difficult to do so close to the broadcast and I asked for an extra rehearsal so that we would be sure to know what we were doing in front of the millions of television viewers.

Then came the night of the telecast.

In every theater, from the Chiabrera to La Scala, everything is rehearsed including the first sets of curtain calls; this is discipline, avoids hurt feelings and trampled feet, and adds order to the backstage chaos. It is normal. At the end of Act III no solo calls were planned, but as the cast regrouped behind the curtain the tenor pushed everyone aside and took his first unscheduled solo call. Lotfi Mansouri, the director, said to himself, "Hey, wait a minute." But he let it go. I asked if we should all take solo calls now but was told no, not to go out.

At the end of the last act, where Gioconda sings the

famous "*Suicidio!*" there was a scheduled solo call which I took and I was met by a standing ovation. Next the director had planned and rehearsed a group call of all the principals, but as we regrouped backstage this man again pushed everyone aside and gave himself another unscheduled solo call. I turned to an official of the San Francisco Opera and asked if there was no discipline in this house, if this was a circus. I was told, "This is his theater and he can do as he pleases here."

I was furious and took no more calls myself, I did not want to play anymore. I hurried to my dressing room and after me came Kurt Herbert Adler and the documentary cameras. All I wanted was to go home, I told Adler. And he said that I should go home to my hotel and I would feel better. That was not what I meant; I wanted to go home to New York, away from all these *gente di merda*, all these shitty people, and that is just what I said. I was appalled at his inefficiency and my reaction was as much against him and his company as against the tenor. The cameras enjoyed this scene, the typical picture of a prima donna throwing a tantrum; but they did not show any of the causes.

Cursing on live television is not something I plan to make a habit of; they were the first words that came to my mind after some very exasperating times. But I am sorry, because *gente di merda* was understood to include too many people in that theater who were in fact blameless. The worst culprit was the theater manager, who permitted the house to be run with such total lack of professionalism and to allow and encourage a tenor to behave so badly to a colleague, to a woman. The other singers had nothing to do with this, and surely the stagehands who were helpful throughout had nothing to do with that man's actions. It was the administration of the company that encouraged these events. The first rehearsal was a sign of things to come, when the tenor had shown up wearing an Arab sheik costume and joking about the current Middle East crisis; the vast kaftan was a cute joke, but it would have been more enjoyable if he had shown up knowing his music and ready to work after the jest.

That night I was outraged because of a singer who is no professional, who turns great art into a joke, who does not work. A star who feels that everything is owed to him but that he owes no respect to his colleagues or to his music. I was sorry that my first *Gioconda* had to be shared with such an unprofessional man. And I was surprised and thrilled when, thanks to Kirk Browning's fabulous direction of the telecast, I was given an Emmy award, the only Emmy given to an opera singer, for my *Gioconda*. I looked at that award not just as a tribute to a fine opera performance but as a reward for my professionalism, for all the suffering I had to put up with in order to sing and act that night. I deserved that Emmy.

After my experiences in San Francisco I confess that I saw all previous stage problems in a new light. It seemed that all of the other bad times in my singing career had been unimportant, and I have been very lucky. I can laugh now at the time when the tenor Giuseppe di Stefano left me alone in the middle of a duet in Donizetti's *L'elisir d'amore* while he sneaked offstage to eat an apple, right during a performance! I was furious then, but now I can laugh: Di Stefano had his quirks, but he was a great singer and, I now understand, a fine colleague.

Then there was the night I almost died in Switzerland. I don't get sick very often, and I rarely cancel a performance. This time I was singing *Un ballo in maschera* in

Zurich and was not feeling my best; I never like to announce that I am sick to ask the audience's indulgence because it hurts their concentration as well as mine and if I am well enough to sing that is all they need to know. So no announcement had been made but I was feeling worse by the minute. As the last act began I had no voice and thought I would faint, so I walked offstage. It is the only time I have ever done that, and it was a horrible feeling. The management didn't have a cover, and there was a two-hour intermission while they waited either to find another soprano or to find me in better form. But the cortisone that I had taken earlier for an infection had somehow made me lose my voice and that was all I could tell them. They accused me of singing only so far but far enough that they would be forced to pay me a full fee. My husband Lorenzo took money out of his pocket and threw their fee back at them. I was so nervous that I took some Valium without Lorenzo seeing me. The doctor came to the dressing room and, not knowing that I had taken the Valium, gave me an injection—also without telling me what it was he had given me. I thought it was more cortisone. It was not. Back at the hotel I drank a bottle of champagne to calm myself. When I went to bed I began to shake; I started to cry. I felt as if I might die. The pills, the shot, the champagne—it's a good thing I did not fall asleep. Finally around 4 A.M. I started to calm down. Lorenzo got the car and we drove right back to Italy before dawn.

More familiar, and worse, than any Swiss virus were the *Callasiani* I encountered in New York. The problem had not surfaced for a while, but it reared its puzzling head during the Met's production of Verdi's *Luisa Miller*. It all happened on the night of a telecast of the opera live from Lincoln Center.

Luisa's first aria comes in the first scene after a very brief recitative. There is a pause before she begins to sing, with her father by her side. . . . "Brava Callas!" I heard somebody shout before I opened my mouth to sing. But I was not alone on that stage; Sherrill Milnes was playing my father, and he offered me his arm, all in character, and I held on to him as I recovered my concentration thanks to him.

Later in the same opera Luisa sings, *"Tu puniscimi, O Signore/se t'offesi e paga sono / ma de barbari al furore / non lasciarmi in abbandono,"* Punish me, O God, if I have offended You, but do not abandon me to the wrath of these barbarians.

The barbarians were just what I had to face in the fall of 1981 for the opening night of the Metropolitan Opera with *Norma.* It was a nightmare. After the long first scene the Druids gather to await their priestess, who will lead them in prayer. Norma's first words, *"Sediziose voci, voci di guerra,"* lead to one of the most beautiful and difficult scenes in all of opera. I had worked hard on this role and I was so happy to sing it in the theater I considered my home. Before I opened my mouth, before I could sing a note, as I stood there alone in the center of the Met's huge stage, the shouting began. "Brava Callas, brava Callas." It was horrible. The fact that it was only four people who were later arrested was no consolation. The evening was ruined. The opening night was ruined. I tried to sing but my confidence had left me and my voice quite completely. I was so unsure of myself that during the cadenza of a duet when a colleague made a musical mistake I was sure that I had made the mistake. I almost cried onstage, right onstage! Where I should have been concentrating totally on the drama, I tried to fight back the tears and support my voice to at least get out the notes. At intermission I cried in my dressing room. I wondered if it was really worth it and I actually thought of just leaving, leaving the performance, leaving the Met, leaving New York. I wanted so much for this nightmare to end. I felt I had no friends. Plácido Domingo was wonderful and considerate, but we were in the same boat, we had both had our opening night spoiled. He told me, "You have to go back out there, Renata. You have to show them who you are. You can't let them beat you. How a handful of people can ruin an opera for four thousand is a sad fact to contemplate." I finished the performance, but there was no Bellini that night; it was a circus that the papers insisted on reviewing as if it were a performance; some even lied and failed to mention that the shouts and boos began before I had had a chance to sing. Suddenly, after my many Normas elsewhere, after a tremendous personal success in Vienna, it was the critical consensus in New York that this was not a role for me. My God, some critics had decided how the evening was going to turn out before the curtain went up. I remember how on September 21, 1981, the morning of the opening— before I had sung one note—the New York *Daily News* ran a feature on the opening of the Met's new season with the banner headline on the front page of the arts section: RENATA SCREECHO TAKES OVER. So much for journalistic objectivity. I also will always remember one critic honest enough to realize that this was one opening night that could not be considered representative, and for a real appreciation of my Norma he should come back to a later performance: Peter G. Davis. In a long review for *New York* magazine on October 5, 1981, he remembered that

". . . come to think of it, booing Normas is something of a Met tradition. Milanov got her share back in 1954, and two years later, Callas was greeted with cries of 'Basta, diva!' " Then the review continued:

> Time and again, Scotto reminded us of her sovereign musicality, her instinctive feeling for the rhythmic integrity of the notes, her ability to mold finely sculpted phrases, and her sensitivity for coloring words into emotions that instantly define a dramatic situation. . . . On a purely dramatic level, Scotto conceives of Norma in classical terms, and her acting was notably restrained and simple. Part of her reserve may have been due to the stress of opening night or her reaction to hostile segments of the audience, but Scotto's concentrated intensity made the dilemma of Bellini's heroine very real. Her position of authority as a Druid high priestess was never in doubt, nor the anguish of her situation as a spurned lover and an unwed mother. With precise economy of means, Scotto presented a woman whose public image had smothered her secret private life, until the end of the opera, when, with one touching gesture, she removed the crown from her head, accepted full responsibility for her actions, and prepared to die. No, Scotto's was not a perfect Norma, but we're not likely to have a better one in the here and now.

Many friends seemed to disappear that opening night, and others kept telling me not to worry, and that only made it worse. I had never felt worse in my life. I had been forced to betray my art; I was not Norma that night, I was a poor woman, humiliated and terrorized and wishing to be a thousand miles away.

The second performance got a standing ovation, and so it went for the rest of the season. I took Norma on tour with the Met that year and the reviews were as favorable as they had been in Europe, even if retractions or second visits seemed mostly out of the question in New York. But frankly that first *Norma* hurt my confidence and it showed in my voice for about a year. So much of singing is concentration, and that requires total confidence in the voice and total attention to the drama. It is not easy to do that in a circus atmosphere, and the results were bound to linger. A friend reminded me of how the great Rosa Ponselle had been so hurt by the abuse that her Carmen took at the Met that she left disillusioned and the world was deprived of Rosa Ponselle's mature genius as a performing artist. He hoped that the same would not happen to me. I hoped not either.

Thirteen

Scotto

I had blood on my hands the first time that we met to discuss writing this book. I was preparing the role of Lady Macbeth for my debut at Covent Garden in 1981. I remember that it was late in the afternoon. I forgot the time as I worked at the piano on *"Una macchia . . . ,"* the Sleepwalking Scene. The final passage leading up to the floated D-flat was giving me trouble; I could not place the note properly. I was singing then when I heard a knock at the door and wished everything away by hitting the music stand by the piano. It hit me back, and I was cut in the forehead. The figure that got up to answer the door was that of a slightly mad woman in leather jeans and silk blouse, holding ice to her forehead and dripping blood. Here, asking if I were all right, was this young critic who had written about my singing in the Washington *Post* and who now wanted to write with me about my life.

Sit down, please, I told him as I returned to the piano and sang the aria with a perfectly floated final D-flat. A public always helps. Now we can talk, I remember telling him.

It was a nice beginning. We talked about *Macbeth* first, of course. You have three sensibilities in this opera, I said. Verdi's romantic music, Shakespeare's Elizabethan play, and a tale that reaches beyond medieval times. There should be no conflict among these if the work is a great one, but the composer is always right. The acting? In opera it should be plain but it should be graphic. How can I sing Lady Macbeth when I am only a Mimi or a Gilda? Simple, I think I can do it. And I love taking risks, my career has been made of them. I could have stopped with five roles and had a great career: Violetta, Lucia, Amina, Butterfly, and perhaps Gilda or Mimi. I could have become known as a phenomenal vocalist in these roles, rested, made lots of money, and lived well. But that would have been boring. Good for the audience up to a point, but they too would get bored. I want audiences to come to me for new ideas, new characters.

How many people hate Scotto, how many adore her? Only by taking chances can I create these extremes, and that is good. Everyone who is someone never stops. Why should a singer stop growing? As for any failed risks, ask the people who don't like me. When I have chosen a new role I have done so with integrity, convinced that it is good for me. I will not announce my forthcoming Isolde or Evita only for the sake of shock. I know what I can do. And I would rather be alone, truly alone, than be surrounded by people who just smile and agree, people who are afraid to speak out whatever the problem may be. They say that I am difficult, but I would rather be difficult than devious. I would rather speak and hear the truth. They say I am controversial. That only means that I like to speak plainly.

When I am told that I am too short to play Tosca, I ask who says that Tosca has to be tall. *Non è l'altezza che fa la grandezza.* I never met Maria Malibran, so Maria Callas was the greatest interpreter I saw when I was becoming a singer. But I tell a true story of how she behaved when we met for the first time and suddenly I cause controversy. Truth offends. I never lie to or about my colleagues. I never run with praise to the dressing room if I cannot mean it, so they believe me whenever I do. I am called controversial too because I sing so many different roles. That is a cliché that has followed me all my life. I never

Preceding page, Donizetti's Anna Bolena, one of his most profound characters, along with Maria di Rohan and Lucia di Lammermoor. (photo: Phil Schexnyder, Dallas) At top, my first Norma, in Turin, directed by Raf Vallone. Bottom right, Bellini's *Zaira*, in its first performance of this century. (photo: Giovanni Consoli, Catania) Bottom left, preparing Cilea's *Adriana Lecouvreur* with Raf Vallone (photo: Caroline Crawford); and as Adriana. (photo: J. Heffernan)

Opposite page, Elisabetta de Valois with two friends in Verdi's *Don Carlo* at the Met. (photo: J. Heffernan)

In creating the role of Lady Macbeth, all of her monstrous cruelty should never be allowed to chill the humanity out of Verdi's music. Opposite and top left at the Met. (photos: J. Heffernan) Top right and bottom at Covent Garden. (photos: Reg Wilson)

At left, Ponchielli's *La Gioconda*. I received an Emmy for my first Gioconda, and I really deserved it for all the grief that came with that production in San Francisco. At right, my first Desdemona, with Jon Vickers as Verdi's Otello. Jon is such a great actor that in the final scene I was truly scared for my life. (photo: J. Heffernan)

Opposite page, *Francesca da Rimini* at the Met. At top, Francesca with her ladies-in-waiting. Bottom, with her lover Paolo, Plácido Domingo. Following page, D'Annunzio's words are easily the most beautiful I have ever sung. (photos: J. Heffernan)

wanted to be forbidden to sing by a fashion that was not the composer's creation. Received tradition always needs renewal.

Do I think of myself as a diva? It's difficult to maintain that attitude, you know. Even after I was anointed with a mink for a Blackglama "What Becomes a Legend Most?" poster, I still had to wash my children's clothes, clean my house, go to the supermarket and pick out the best vegetables. A diva would not drive her own car, or scream at the children when they misbehave, or take care of her family. I don't fool around with singing when I am at home, I have too much to do. It might be easy to play at being a diva, but that's not for me.

The conversation stopped when our friend Jonathan Pell dropped in to deliver my Emmy award for *La Gioconda*. We have to talk about this, I said, holding the golden statue. We have to talk about so many things.

A few weeks later we were in a limousine going from the Kennedy Center to my hotel following a *Manon Lescaut* with the Met on tour. It was a huge black car. A friend of mine, I said, told me a long time ago that I would have one of these cars and I didn't believe him. It's as big as our room in Savona where I grew up. You should see Savona now; the city has gotten so big, sometimes I don't recognize it. It seems so very long ago, the war, how hungry, how really hungry we were. We have to talk.

And we had many conversations in the next three years, in Italy, in New York, on tour. We talked about the future, about *Werther* and *La clemenza di Tito*, *La fanciulla del West*, *Carmen*. We talked about recitals, about finding hidden works of Rossini, Verdi, Respighi and offering them to an audience. I would like to sing more recitals now and less opera, I would like to have time to sing in

different languages. Imagine, to sing Chopin or Tchaikovsky! In opera I become the character I portray, I am always someone else. In recitals I am I, Renata Scotto,
singer. I am completely exposed as an instrument, as a
woman. It has not been easy to balance a career and a
family, but I cannot imagine one without the other. A
woman should not have to choose. As a child I had so little
that I wanted everything when I grew up. I think I have
done well. The only truly terrible times are when I find
myself wishing that I were only one thing or the other. I
remember one time when my children were in New York
and I was singing *Manon Lescaut* in Bonn. The premiere
finished at eleven, then there was dinner with many fans,
and around three in the morning I returned to my hotel
exhausted. My children, awake in New York, thought
nothing of calling me to settle a fight they were having
with the baby-sitter about what to do that day. I was
sleepy and tired and felt a lecture on time difference coming; but I am their mother and I can't just say, "Don't
bother me, I have to rest so I can work." They were so far
away. Of course I listened to my children and settled their
trouble, but why couldn't I be just a singer and nothing
else for one night? It was an awful feeling. The opposite is
just as bad, as when in San Francisco I wished to simply
go home to my family and away from all those people. Of
course I stayed and sang, but at that point I simply wanted
to be home with Laura, Filippo, and Lorenzo and never
sing again. Neither of those extremes is really the way I
am. Music, and love too, cannot be just somewhere you
drop in for a visit, all dressed up for the occasion. You
have to live there. Everything that I am—singer, lover,
mother—is reflected in every part of my life. The joy of

my singing brought me and my husband together, and the joy of my husband and children has kept me singing. And within that there is a small part that is private, and that is how it should remain.

Discography

The following discography lists nearly one hundred
records by Renata Scotto, all of her commercial recordings
as well as a selection of easily obtainable private recordings, for which the date of performance is given. When a
recording is available in more than one label, the domestic
(U.S.A.) label is given unless there is a marked difference
in the sound quality of the pressings, in which case usually
the English or German label is indicated. An appendix
listing selected videotaped television performances follows
the discography.—O.R.

VINCENZO BELLINI (1801–35)

I Capuleti e i Montecchi.   Renata Scotto, Giacomo Aragall, Agostino Ferrin, Alfredo Giacomotti. Claudio Abbado, cond. La Scala, January 8, 1968 (live). *MRF-55.*

Norma.   Renata Scotto, Tatiana Troyanos, Giuseppe Giacomini, Paul Plishka, Ann Murray, Paul Crook. Ambrosian Opera Chorus, National Philharmonic Orch., James Levine, cond. *CBS M3 35902.*

La Sonnambula.   Renata Scotto, Alfredo Kraus, Ivo Vinco, Rosa Laghezza, Marisa Zotti. Nello Santi, cond. La Fenice, May 26, 1961 (live). *HRE-337-2.*

La Sonnambula   (scenes). Renata Scotto, Stuart Burrows, Forbes Robinson, Heather Begg, Jill Gomez, George MacPherson. Carlo Felice Cillario, cond. Covent Garden, March 20, 1971 (live). *MRF-132(4).*

La Straniera.   Renata Scotto, Renato Cioni, Enrico Campi, Elena Zilio, Domenico Trimarchi, Maurizio Mazzieri, Glauco Scarlini. Nino Zanzogno, cond. Palermo, December 10, 1968 (live). *MRF-30.*

Zaira.   Renata Scotto, Luigi Roni, Maria Luisa Nave, Giorgio Casellato-Lamberti, Giovanna Collica, Mario Rinaudi, Nino Valori, Carmelo Mollica. Danilo Belardinelli, cond. Teatro Massimo Bellini, Catania, March 30, 1976 (live). *BJR 146-3.*

Zaira. Same cast as above. April 1, 1976 (live). *MRF 132(3); MRF 132(4).*

Renata Scotto's international career was launched by Bellini's music, but to date only one commercial operatic recording has been made of the soprano's favorite field of specialization. Several private recordings exist, fortunately; and in varying degrees of listenability they document some of Scotto's finest moments onstage. The CBS *Norma* is a success in almost every respect; here, as onstage, Scotto's Norma is no verismo trumpet but a woman first and foremost. The impact is in her lyricism, and even the top As in *"Casta diva"* show their strength only through veils of feminine dignity: the barbarian, the lover, the mother are all in the music, which is sung throughout in the original keys (Scotto and Troyanos were the first Norma and Adalgisa in the Metropolitan Opera House's history to sing Act II as Bellini wrote it). Troyanos does not blend well with Scotto in purely vocal terms, but the warmth and sympathy between the two characters has rarely been so audible. Only in *"Mira, O Norma"* does one miss a soprano's timbre in Adalgisa—a revelation that may be heard in Scotto's duet recording with Mirella Freni (see MISCELLANEOUS RECITALS). *"In mia man"* is a lesson in dramatic singing within the bel canto parameters. Levine's conducting is light-years ahead of his first recording of the opera, and the whole affair is a magnificent souvenir of one of the soprano's most ambitious and successful creations.

   I Capuleti e i Montecchi is unusually well produced for a private record; indeed, it is the best available recording of Bellini's tale of Romeo and Juliet available in any form. The evening marked Scotto's return to La Scala after an absence of three years, and from the sound of this record it was a splendid homecoming. Juliet's entrance, in Act I, Scene 2, set the tone for the performance: *"Eccomi in veste . . ."* mocks the girl's fine costume in a veiled voice that Scotto does not often use, gradually becoming clearer and clearer in the recitative until the delicate embellishments that caress the words as the flames of a funeral pyre on the phrase *"per me faci ferali."* A strong vocal wind sweeps through the word *"Ardo,"* and only then is Juliet's proper entrance allowed to begin in full, luscious voice on the famous aria *"Oh, quante volte."* It was Scotto's idea to use a tenor Romeo for the first time, and her choice of Aragall certainly makes a good case for the sex change from Bellini's original: he sings in the correct keys, embellishes modestly but well within the style, and the vocal blend of the two young lovers is ideal. Abbado's conducting shows an affinity for bel canto that would not be evident in later years.

The *Sonnambula* recordings are not in very good sound, but the Venice performance with Kraus is well worth seeking out. Five years after Edinburgh, Scotto had found her way out of tradition and into her unique bel canto sensibility: every note Amina sings is colored by the words and never allowed to soar into sheer virtuosity. Most striking on the recording are the audible contrasts between Amina's sleeping and waking hours, and the shock the young girl experiences on finding herself suddenly awake in strange surroundings. More than the lovely pastel that this opera can become on records and in the opera house, this *Sonnambula* is moving in its pathos and simplicity. The scenes from the 1971 *Sonnambula* mark the soprano's return to Covent Garden after six years; separated by a decade from the Venice recording, Scotto's voice is both lighter and more fiery in this production, scenes of which are included only in earlier pressings of the MRF *Zaira* marked 132(4); later packages do not include this bonus record.

La Straniera was a turning point for Scotto, a signpost leading to *Norma;* this recording shows fine vocal characterization but none of the principals was in his or her best voice for the occasion, and the recorded sound is flat.

Zaira did capture the singers in fine shape (on both nights! Surely it is a bit excessive to have private recordings of the same production three days apart). Much of the music of *Zaira* made its way in exalted fashion to *I Capuleti e i Montecchi,* but it is interesting to hear the composer's first thoughts in this abandoned opera. The BJR pressings are as usual better than those of MRF, with the excitement of opening night giving an extra attraction to that set; the orchestra does not begin betraying signs of rehearsal until the second performance, however.

ALFREDO CATALANI (1854–93)

La Wally. Renata Tebaldi, Renata Scotto, Mario del Monaco, Giorgio Tozzi, Jolanda Gardino, Gian Giacomo Guelfi, Melchiore Luise. Carlo Maria Giulini, cond. La Scala, December 7, 1953 (live). *HRE-382-2.*

This recording is a document of Renata Scotto's debut at La Scala and it is fascinating in several ways. First it is easy to hear why the twenty-year-old soprano garnered twice as many curtain calls in the secondary trouser role of Walter as the more experienced and famous leading soprano and tenor. But second and most interesting is that in this live performance of 1953 we have the only recorded Scotto interpretation which does not sound like Scotto; she lightens the voice in a way that cannot be attributed only to age, and one can at least understand if not agree with those who put her in the Dal Monte and Pagliughi soubrette camp at this stage of her career. The performances are very good, although Tebaldi is heard to better advantage in her commercial recording of the opera; the sound is awful even by pirate standards.

LUIGI CHERUBINI (1760–1842)

Medea. Maria Callas, Renata Scotto, Miriam Pirazzini, Mirto Picchi, Giuseppe Modesti, Linda Marimpietri, Elvira Galassi, Alfredo Giacomotti. La Scala Chorus and Orch., Tulio Serafin, cond. *Ricordi AOCL 316001; Everest-Cetra S-437/3; Mercury STR 90000.*

This is Scotto's first commercial recording, singing the role of Glauce opposite Callas's Medea. The first sessions began the morning after Scotto's Edinburgh *Sonnambula,* where she gained international acclaim by taking Callas's place on three days' notice. The young soprano certainly acquitted herself quite well in this record as well. The suggestion was made during the sessions that Glauce's music be cut, but Maestro Serafin refused and his decision was a fortunate one: Glauce's first-act aria *"O amore, vieni a me!"* is for once more than an interlude while we wait for the sorceress' entrance, and the narration and trio that follow show an unassuming, lovely grasp of this most innocent pawn of the tragedy. It is also revelatory to hear the growth of the voice and the artist herself between the dramatic sounds made here and the lovely but shallower virtuosity of the boy Walter in *La Wally.*

FRANCESCO CILÈA (1866–1950)

Adriana Lecouvreur. Renata Scotto, Plácido Domingo, Elena Obraztsova, Giancarlo Luccardi, Florindo Andreoli, Lillian Watson, Ann Murray, Paul Crook, Paul Hudson. Ambrosian Opera Chorus, Philharmonia Orch., James Levine, cond. *CBS M3 34588.*

Adriana Lecouvreur (scenes). Renata Scotto, José Carreras. 1978? (live). *HRE-351-2.*

This is one of Scotto's great roles and one of her best records. The collaboration with Levine, Domingo, Milnes, and Obraztsova lift Cilèa's opera out of the critical condescension in which it was held for so long; and if no recording can prove *Adriana* to be a masterpiece, this one does reveal its great dramatic power. Scotto does this through the music first and last, in a beautifully *sung* interpretation that purposely stays away from melodramatic exaggerations, excessive portamenti, or dynamic liberties; she and Levine never fail to convey the constant pulse of the work with bel canto insistence. The recitation at the opening has never been more clearly drawn, the aria *"Io son l'umile ancella"* manages to sound autobiographical echoes in its revelatory treatment, and the death of Adriana has the immediacy of a stage performance—an achievement ranking with Scotto's two *Butterfly* recordings. The duets with

Carreras are uncredited and legally risky souvenirs of what was a genial pairing on the Met stage; Scotto is rhythmically a bit freer than in the studio recording, but it is a tribute to CBS and its artists that the commercial recording has no reason to envy the live performance in terms of dramatic immediacy. Carreras is of course wonderful, and it would be a difficult choice indeed to pick the better of the two Maurizios.

GAETANO DONIZETTI (1797–1848)

Anna Bolena. Renata Scotto, Tatiana Troyanos, Umberto Grilli, Ezio Flagello, Nancy Williams, Nicola Zaccaria, Piero de Palma. Fernando Previtali, cond. Dallas?, 1975 (live, uncredited). *HRE-348-3.*

L'elisir d'amore. Renata Scotto, Carlo Bergonzi, Fernando Corena. Franceso Molinari-Pradelli, cond. Metropolitan Opera?, 1968 (live, uncredited). *HRE-315-2.*

L'elisir d'amore. Renata Scotto, Giuseppe di Stefano, Giulio Fioravanti, Ivo Vinco, Luisa Rossi. Gianandrea Gavazzeni, cond. Teatro G. Donizetti, Bergamo, October 14, 1961 (live). *Warner-Movimento Musica 03.009.*

Lucia di Lammermoor. Renata Scotto, Giuseppe di Stefano, Ettore Bastianini, Ivo Vinco, Franco Ricciardi, Stefania Malagù. La Scala Chorus and Orch., Nino Sanzogno, cond. *Ricordi AOCL 216004; DG SLMP 13870415; Everest-Cetra S-439/2.*

Lucia di Lammermoor. Renata Scotto, Piero Cappuccilli, Agostino Ferrin, Franco Ricciardi, Anna di Stasio,

Gianfranco Manganotti. RAI-Turin, Francesco Molinari-Pradelli, cond. 1968 (live). *HRE-361-2.*

Maria di Rohan. Renata Scotto, Umberto Grilli, Renato Bruson, Flora Rafanelli, Paolo Cesari, Karl Schreiber, Neron Ceron, Alessandro Cassis. Gianandrea Gavazzeni, cond. La Fenice, March 20, 1974 (live). *MRF-103.*

The Ricordi *Lucia di Lammermoor* was Scotto's first chance to record with La Scala and with Di Stefano, so she thought it best not to turn it down even though she had not yet sung the role onstage. Perhaps it was too early. The vocalism is admirable and the voice is fresh, but that is all; at times she seems to be reading the music for the first time. The 1968 RAI recording is more representative of the celebrated Scotto Lucia, with each word carefully colored and each mood conveyed through the vocal line. Still, in the Cetra set *"Regnava nel silenzio"* has delicate trills that suggest themselves rather than pointing to their tonal borders, and the singing is informed with a simplicity that would soon be joined by dramatic impact. The difficulties of the recording sessions to accommodate Di Stefano's unusual hours are rarely heard. The RAI performance has no Di Stefano, of course; it is also horribly cut, with virtually no music left between the sextet and the Mad Scene. *Anna Bolena* is a revelation, particularly in the staggering final scene and in the duet with Troyanos, as the doomed queen appears first in devotion, then in wrath, and finally in the most profoundly sad feeling of forgiveness and acceptance. *Maria di Rohan* was originally intended as a vehicle for Scotto at La Scala, but the birth of her son Filippo changed those plans; she sang in the production later in Venice and in Lisbon. The recording has modest sound, but there is much musical and dramatic wealth to be found in this neglected score; Scotto and Gavazzeni work as one, especially in the aria *"Cupa, fatal mestizia"* and in the final trio, where more effective Donizetti scores are brought to mind. The *Elisir* from 1968, an uncredited Met performance, is one of Scotto's most delicate characterizations, apparently not bothered at all by her being four months pregnant at the time; it is only surpassed by the 1961 Bergamo performance, in which the deliberate tempo and phrasing of Adina's opening recitatives speak volumes of her flirtatious nature.

UMBERTO GIORDANO (1867–1948)

Andrea Chénier. Renata Scotto, Plácido Domingo, Sherrill Milnes, Jean Kraft, Maria Ewing, Michel Sénechal, Allan Monk, Enzo Dara, Gwendolyn Killebrew, Stuart Harling, Terence Sharp, Piero de Palma, Malcolm King. John Alldis Choir, National Philharmonic Orch., James Levine, cond. *RCA ARL-3-2046.*

Maddalena is not a very important role for Scotto, but here she makes a lovely impression, discreet and feminine, refreshingly straightforward in the final duet on the way to the guillotine. Domingo is the best Chénier on records, and James Levine seems to breathe along with his singers.

CHARLES GOUNOD (1818–93)

Faust. Renata Scotto, Alfredo Kraus, Nicolai Ghiaurov, Lorenzo Saccomani, Milena Dal Piva, Anna di Stasio, Guido Mazzini. NKH Orch. and Chorus, Paul Ethuin, cond. Tokyo, September 9, 1973 (live). *HRE-345-3(S).*

Faust. Renata Scotto, Eugenio Fernandi, Nicola Rossi-Lemeni, Piero Guelfi, Vincenzo Preziosa, Clara Betner, Anna Maria Anelli. RAI Turin, Armando La Rosa Parodi, cond., July 15, 1960 (live). *Warner-Movimento Musica 03.003.*

Filèmone e Bauci. Renata Scotto, Jolanda Torriani, Alvinio Misciano, Rolando Panerai, Paolo Montarsolo. RAI Milan, Nino Sanzogno, cond. May 7, 1961 (live). *Foyer 1027(2)* (available in the United States through the German News Company).

Filèmone e Bauci. selections. Same performance as above, mislabeled as a 1957 broadcast. *LR-155.*

Neither Scotto nor Kraus has recorded *Faust* commercially, so this Japanese television sound track is indispensable. The stereo sound is very good and so are the HRE pressings. Marguerite's fascination with the tempting jewelry is almost childlike in Scotto's voice, making her transfiguration in the final trio all the more satisfying. Fernandi is no Kraus, and the 1960 performance is sung in Italian translation; yet the earlier set is also captivating and comparison of the two says much about the so-called darkening of the Scotto instrument over the years: her Marguerite is vocally lighter, more supple and playful in the Jewel Song in Tokyo in 1973 than in Turin thirteen years earlier, suggesting that the heavier sound of recent years is not so much due to maturing as to the choice of roles; and that the lightness, as in the 1973 *Faust* or the 1983 stage performances of *Manon* in Chicago, can be summoned at command. *Filèmone e Bauci* is one of the few private records that Scotto likes, and the complete and better-pressed European import is preferable to the abridged Legendary Recording edition. Gounod's fantasy to a libretto by Barbier and Carré deserves to be better known, and the sweetness of this recorded performance could do much to serve its cause. Scotto's transformation from young girl to old woman to young girl, and her begging the god Giove to return her old age again, all come through clearly in her voice.

RUGGIERO LEONCAVALLO (1858–1919)

I Pagliacci. Renata Scotto, José Carreras, Kari Nurmela, Ugo Benelli, Thomas Allen. Southend Boys' Choir, Philharmonia Orch., Riccardo Muti, cond. 1978 *EMI 1C 165-03 800/2* (German News); *Angel SZX-3895.*

Scotto sang the role of Nedda only at the beginning of her career, but the memories seem to have been strong enough to carry overflowing emotions to this 1978 recording. The woman's cruelty and her frustration are audible, and impeccably sung; and there are dramatic echoes in the characterization of the air of desperation that hangs over Puccini's *Il Tabarro*. Muti's tempos are calculated where they should be crisp, and his cool approach here works against the drama. Carreras is surprisingly strong while remaining very lyric in sound.

PIETRO MASCAGNI (1863–1945)

Cavalleria Rusticana. Renata Scotto, Plácido Domingo, Isola Jones, Jean Kraft, Anne Simon. Ambrosian Opera Chorus, National Philharmonic Orch., James Levine, cond. *RCA RL-13091*.

One of James Levine's finest achievements on records, this *Cavalleria* boasts the best dramatic singing of this work available. Domingo is a much stronger vocal and dramatic presence than in his first recording; and Scotto, although Santuzza is not her role, creates an unforgettable portrait almost recalling the old verismo tradition in its generous use of glottal drops and rhythmic flexibility, yet always sung to the letter as the composer wrote it.

GIACOMO MEYERBEER (1791–1864)

Le Prophète. Marilyn Horne, Renata Scotto, James McCracken, Jerome Hines, Jules Bastin, Christian du Plessis, Jean Dupouy. Ambrosian Opera Chorus, Royal Philharmonic Orch., Henry Lewis, cond. *Columbia M4-34340*.

Roberto il diavolo. Renata Scotto, Stefania Malagù, Boris Christoff, Gianfranco Manganotti, Giovanni

Antonini, Marisa Sansoni, Ottavio Taddei. Nino
Sanzogno, cond. Maggio Musicale Fiorentino, May
7, 1968 (live). *MRF-20.*

It was a luxury to have Scotto sing Berthe to Horne's
Fidès, much as it was a luxury to have Horne sing the Zia
to Scotto's recorded Suor Angelica. Would that more recording firms followed that policy. *Le Prophète* is a grand
vehicle for the considerable talent of Marilyn Horne, and
Scotto is not likely to repeat the role of Berthe onstage
again; on records, it is thrilling to have the *echt* Scotto
coloratura of *"Mon coeur s'élance et palpite"* in the first scene,
to have a recreation of the wild Meyerbeerian mad scene
that brought the soprano such acclaim at the Met in John
Dexter's production. *Roberto il diavolo* is a live recording of
the opening of the Maggio Musicale Fiorentino in 1968,
and with some reservations it can be called an excellent
recording of the role of Isabella. The reservations are that
the grandeur has been shorn off this grand opera by a
cruel editor's hand: while the part of Isabella is sung by
Scotto in its entirety, all the other principal roles have
been cut into disfigurement. The Italian translation here,
unlike that of Gounod's *Faust* and *Filèmone e Bauci,* leaves
much to be desired. It is a record for fans of Scotto but not
necessarily for fans of Meyerbeer.

GIOVANNI BATTISTA PERGOLESI (1710–36)

La serva padrona. Renata Scotto, Sesto Bruscantini. I Virtuosi di Roma, Renato Fasano, cond. *Ricordi-Mercury
SR-90240.*

A delicious performance, recorded with care at the Teatro Grande in Brescia. Sesto Bruscantini has none of the buffo excesses that can overwhelm this Pergolesi miniature; the Virtuosi di Roma have all the virtues of the best early-music ensembles and none of their academic fastidiousness. And Renata Scotto's comic characterization is a treat, funny and delightful, sung in the freshest and naughtiest of voices. The recording has gone in and out of print several times, and it is worth searching for.

GIACOMO PUCCINI (1858–1924)

La Bohème. Renata Scotto, Gianni Poggi, Jolanda Meneguzzer, Tito Gobbi, Giorgio Giorgetti, Giuseppe Modesti, Virgilio Carbonari, Enzo Guagni, Mario Frosini, Augusto Frati. Antonino Votto, cond. Maggio Musicale Fiorentino. *DG 2705038.*

La Bohème. Renata Scotto, Alfredo Kraus, Sherrill Milnes, Matteo Manuguerra, Paul Plishka, Renato Capecchi, Italo Tajo, Carol Neblett, Paul Crook, Michael Lewis, John Noble. Trinity Boys' Choir, Ambrosian Opera Chorus, National Philharmonic Orch., James Levine, cond. *EMI 1C 165-03807/08* (German News); *Angel SZBX-3900.*

La Bohème (scenes). Renata Scotto, José Carreras. Metropolitan Opera (?), 1977 (live, uncredited). *HRE-351.*

Edgar. Renata Scotto, Carlo Bergonzi, Gwendolyn Killebrew, Vicente Sardinero. Opera Orch. of New York, Eve Queler, cond. *Columbia M2-34584.*

Madama Butterfly. Renata Scotto, Carlo Bergonzi, Rolando Panerai, Piero de Palma, Giuseppe Morresi, Paolo Montarsolo, Mario Rinaudo. Rome Opera Chorus and Orch., Sir John Barbirolli, cond. *EMI 1C 157 00081/83* (German News); *Angel S-3702.*

Madama Butterfly. Renata Scotto, Plácido Domingo, Ingvar Wixell, Gillian Knight, Florindo Andreolli, Malcolm King, Ann Murray, Jonathan Summers, Leslie Fyson, Christopher Keyte, Alan Byers, Gloria Jennings, Jean Temperley, Linda Richardson. Ambrosian Opera Chorus, Philharmonia Orch., Lorin Maazel, cond. *CBS M3-35181.*

Madama Butterfly (scenes). Renata Scotto, José Carreras. San Francisco (?) 1974 (live. uncredited). *HRE-351.*

Tosca. Renata Scotto, Plácido Domingo, Renato Bruson, John Cheek, Renato Capecchi, Andrea Velis, Paul Hudson, Itzhak Perlman. Ambrosian Opera Chorus, St. Clement Danes School Boys' Choir, Philharmonia Orch., James Levine, cond. *EMI 1C 165-03955/56* (German News); *Angel DSX-3919(D).*

Suor Angelica. Renata Scotto, Marilyn Horne, Ileana Cotrubas, Patricia Payne, Gillian Knight, Ann Howard, Doreen Cryer, Margaret Cable, Elizabeth Bainbridge, Shirley Minty, Gloria Jennings, Della Jones. Ambrosian Opera Chorus, New Philharmonia Orch., Lorin Maazel, cond. *CBS M-34505;* also in *Il Trittico* set *CBS M3-35192.*

Il Tabarro. Renata Scotto, Plácido Domingo, Ingvar Wixell, Michel Sénechal, Gillian Knight, Dennis Wicks, John Treleaven, Yvonne Kenny, Peter Jeffes. Ambrosian Opera Chorus, Philharmonia Orch., Lorin

Maazel, cond. *CBS M-34570(Q)*; also in *Il Trittico* set *CBS M3-35192.*

Turandot. Birgit Nilsson, Renata Scotto, Franco Corelli, Bonaldo Giaiotti, Piero de Palma. Rome Opera Chorus and Orch., Francesco Molinari-Pradelli, cond. *EMI SLS-921; EMI 1C 165-0-00050/2* (German News); Angel S-3671.

Le Villi. Renata Scotto, Plácido Domingo, Leo Nucci, Tito Gobbi. Ambrosian Opera Chorus, National Philharmonic Orch., Lorin Maazel, cond. *CBS M-36669.*

If her place in musical history is secure for her bel canto interpretations as well as for her definitive Verdi heroines, it is for her verismo that Renata Scotto will be remembered as the model for generations to come; for it is she who has put the music back into the repertory of this period. After years of tradition ossifying upon tradition, of melodramatic excesses and posturing onstage, here is a woman who has heightened the drama and cleansed the style, setting it on the right path simply by trusting the composer and following his score. Her records of verismo operas display this power to the last one, and none is as essential as her recordings of Puccini. The two *Butterfly* recordings are her best among these.

With other operas that Renata Scotto has recorded more than once there is usually a clear choice among the offerings; this is not so with *Madama Butterfly*. Each recording is unique, each is thoroughly Puccinian. In each there is Cio-Cio-San the woman, not the doll or even the young girl, for this is a woman who has seen much by the age of fifteen. Her entrance is touching in its insistence on forced happiness, in the indications of the young bride's desperation and fear. "Barbirolli has an Italian brain," Scotto says, and he certainly knows the Puccini idiom. When it appeared, the Barbirolli *Butterfly* was without a doubt the best on records, and its only competition came twenty years later from the same heroine under Maestro Maazel. If anything, the second recording is even more devastating in its emotional impact, more musically correct. Growth in the characterization the soprano attributes to being a mother in real life by the time of the Maazel *Butterfly;* the musical simplicity is an example of Scotto's cleansing of the verismo style. Vocally she is at least as splendid in the Maazel recording, with added details especially in the duets with Sharpless and with Suzuki: Cio-Cio-San can be heard to ignore the oppressive reality, she is desperate to change the topic of conversation with the American, she does not want to see the letter he brings. One can almost see her holding up the child Trouble as a last reckless measure to delay the end; and the end itself captures on records what has been legendary in the theater. It is Scotto's most profound interpretation on records, and her most beautiful singing. These *Butterfly* recordings rank with the Furtwängler-Flagstad *Tristan und Isolde* and the Karajan-Schwarzkopf *Der Rosenkavalier* as among the finest moments in the history of the phonograph.

The recorded *Bohèmes* tell a different story. The first one is an exasperating recording, and it is not surprising that it is Scotto's least favorite of all her records. The soprano is in lovely, fresh voice, but the portrayal is a bit generalized. Poggi's *"Dammi il braccio, mia piccina"* contains some of the ugliest tenor sounds ever put on vinyl, and of course he strains to produce the unwritten high ending of the Act I duet. Vulgar and provincial would not be inappropriate terms to describe the overall performance, down to Votto. Still, this Mimi does sound like a fallen adolescent, and Poggi's impetuous poet does have some crude charm. The second *Bohème*, on the other hand, is a powerful music drama. James Levine's unabashed, unrestrained romanticism never loses control of the musical forces, all the principals are in gorgeous voice, and Scotto's Mimi seems to float her anguish through some of her most delicate singing on records. Kraus's Rodolfo frankly could use some of Poggi's vulgarity, but if the Spaniard's Puccini at best shows great Verdi style, that is nothing to complain about. The Act III ensemble is the clearest on records, thanks to Levine, turning *"Addio, senza rancor"* into the climax, the sad centerpiece of the opera.

The *Tosca*, which received numerous awards in its European release, is another such achievement. It was recorded in long takes and in each act it thunders in one crash from beginning to end; for once *"Vissi d'arte"* does not stop the action but becomes very much one more thread of the melodramatic cloth, and for all its strength the singing remains first and last musical, never resorting to easy parlando or histrionic tricks. In this *Tosca*, the drama is in the music and only in the music. *Suor Angelica* and *Il Tabarro* followed the same policy of very long takes, and the impact is almost as immediate as it is onstage; one can only wonder why CBS did not go ahead and complete *Il Trittico* with Scotto, after having definitive recordings of two of its three operas with the soprano. The final scene of *Suor Angelica* achieves what is quite rare: an expression of religious ecstasy that is instantly communicated to believers and unbelievers alike; it is a figure so sublime as to have been sculpted by Bernini—and it is all in Puccini's

score, to which Scotto is totally faithful. The *Edgar* recording follows the soprano's preferred method for commit-
ting roles to records: a well-engineered but completely live
recording. *Edgar* is a curious opera, Puccinian but still
enough of a hybrid to be close to a posed bel canto style;
Scotto is ideal for it, and the performance is fresh; the last
final scene of this early Puccini jewel foreshadows his last,
Turandot. The EMI recording of *Turandot,* with Birgit
Nilsson, Franco Corelli, and Scotto, is widely considered
to be the best recorded performance of Puccini's swan
song, and certainly it contains the finest portrayal of his
last completed heroine, the slave Liù. This is a womanly
creation, and Liù's entrance has never been so urgent or
sensuous. Uniting frailty and courage and never straying
from the printed score, Scotto bends the notes and time
itself in *"Signore, ascolta,"* shy and hesitating on the first
phrase, bursting with emotion at the close.

LICINIO REFICE (1883–1954)

Cecilia. Renata Scotto, Harry Theyard, Thomas Palmer,
 Gwynn Cornell, Dimitri Kavrakos, Alan Monk, Boris Martinovich, Stephan Algie. Angelo Campori,
 cond. New York 1976, (live). *HRE-244.*

A souvenir of a too rare collaboration between Scotto and
the Italian conductor Angelo Campori. Scotto and
Theyard give impassioned readings of this late verismo
curiosity, but the sound of the private record is boxy and
distant.

NICOLAI RIMSKY-KORSAKOV (1844–1908)

The Invisible City of Ktezh. Renata Scotto, Anna Maria Anelli, Renato Gavarini, Piero Guelfi; Franco Capuana, cond. Trieste, January 12, 1957 (live). *HRE-Impresario* (forthcoming).

GIOACCHINO ROSSINI (1792–1868)

La cambiale di matrimonio. Renata Scotto, Renato Capecchi, Mario Petri, Rolando Panerai, Nicola Monti, Giovanna Fioroni. I Virtuosi di Roma, Renato Fasano, cond. *Ricordi OCL 16044/45; Everest-Cetra S 446/2.*

Giovanna d'Arco (cantata). Renata Scotto; Walter Baracchi, piano. *RCA AGL-1-1341.*

Giovanna d'Arco (cantata). Renata Scotto. Brooklyn Academy of Music, October 25, 1969 (live). *Robin Hood RHR 519-C.*

Petite Messe Solennelle. Renata Scotto, Alfredo Kraus, Fiorenza Cossotto, Ivo Vinco; Franco Verganti and Gianluigi Franz, piano; Luigi Benedetti, organ. Polyphonic Chorus of Milan, Giulio Bertoca, cond. *Ricordi AOCL 216010; Everest-Cetra S-441/2.*

Soirées Musicales. Renata Scotto, Bianca Maria Casoni, Giuseppe Nait, Teodoro Rovetta; Antonio Beltrami, piano. *Deutsche Harmonia Mundi 1C 065-99868.*

La cambiale di matrimonio and the *Petite Messe Solennelle* were recorded in 1960 in Brescia and Florence, continuing the happy collaboration between Scotto and the Virtuosi di Roma. *La Cambiale* was done with Scotto at the insistence of Nanni Ricordi, and it is a gem of the buffo repertory. Scotto's Fanny is light and airy, with much use of a flute-like top that she would not often reveal. Her aria *"Vorrei spiegarvi il giubilo,"* which turned up later as part of the Rosina-Figaro duet in *The Barber of Seville,* is a good example of how Scotto could sing Rossini in a valid and exciting style that was not at all like her Donizetti or Bellini. The *Petite Messe* was written in Paris in 1864 and received its first performance in 1869 on what would have been Rossini's seventy-eighth birthday. It is a small but important masterpiece, and from the pulse of its opening piano figures through the powerful close, it is an operatic, serious, and very lively religious work. The recording is at present difficult to find, but it is worth the search because none since then has been as idiomatic or as moving, and none has been as well sung. In particular it is fascinating to hear the similarity of technique of the two young Llopart pupils, Scotto and Kraus, blending in bel canto splendor with ease and dramatic conviction. The cantata *Giovanna d'Arco* is an Italian counterpart to Beethoven's *Ah, perfido,* and a powerful glimpse into moments of the life of the warrior saint of Orlèans. Both recordings were made shortly after Scotto introduced the work to the United States in her 1969 Carnegie Hall concert; and the studio performance with Walter Baracchi at the piano is the preferred choice of these two. It is a tour de force for Scotto, who gave the cantata its first performance in our century in the legendary recital at La Scala that also included Rossini's *Soirées Musicales.* The recording of the *Soi-*

reés happily is back in print, and although they have been much recorded in part by many great singers of diverse artistic temperaments, from Anna Moffo to Joan Sutherland, none sounds as Rossinian, as Italian, as Scotto in these lovely readings.

GASPARO SPONTINI (1774–1851)

La Vestale (scenes). Renata Scotto, Oralia Domínguez, Graziano del Vivo. Vittorio Gui, cond. Maggio Musicale Fiorentino, May 9, 1970. Included in *MRF-124-S.*

This is a fiftieth-anniversary production of the Maggio Musicale, recalling the first season's Vestale, Rosa Ponselle, and using not only the same sets but also the same conductor, Vittorio Gui. Scotto is regal, in dark and imperious voice and severe classical discretion. The sound is not very good, however, which may partly explain why MRF included only scenes of this production as an appendix to a rather bland performance from a complete RAI broadcast.

GIUSEPPE VERDI (1813–1901)

Un ballo in maschera. Renata Scotto, Leo Nucci, Kathleen Battle, Patricia Payne. Chicago Lyric Opera, 1980, Sir John Pritchard, cond. (live, uncredited). *HRE-821-3(S)* (withdrawn from market).

Un ballo in maschera (scenes). Same cast as above, but with Scotto's arias only: see *Macbeth LR-159(S)* below.

I Lombardi. Renata Scotto, Ruggero Raimondi, Umberto Grilli, Anna di Stasio, Mario Rinaudo, Alfredo Colella, Fernando Jacopucci, Sofia Mezzetti. Gianandrea Gavazzeni, cond. Rome Opera, November 20, 1969 (live). *Robin Hood RHR-519-C.*

I Lombardi (scenes). Renata Scotto, José Carreras, Paul Plishka, Franco Marini, Annette Parler, Will Roy, Yoshi Ito. Sarah Lawrence College Chorus, Opera Orch. of New York, Eve Queler, cond., 1972. *BJR-S-132;* highlights in *HRE-351.*

Macbeth. Renata Scotto, Sherrill Milnes, Giuliano Ciannella, John Cheek, Timothy Jenkins, Carol Dorman, Joseph Moore, Peter Merrick, Virgil Cabot, Guido Canale, Laura Carney, George Martins. Chicago Symphony Orch., James Levine, cond. Ravinia Festival, 1981 (live, uncredited). *HRE-398-3(S).*

Macbeth (scenes). Renata Scotto, Renato Bruson. Riccardo Muti, cond. Covent Garden, 1981 (live, uncredited). Side 2 includes scenes from *Un ballo in maschera* John Pritchard, cond. Chicago, 1980 (live, uncredited). *LR-159(S).*

Messa da Requiem. Renata Scotto, Agnes Baltsa, Veriano Luchetti, Yevgeni Nesterenko. Ambrosian Opera Chorus, Philharmonia Orch., Riccardo Muti, cond. *EMI 1C-165-03653/54* (German News); *Angel SZ-3858.*

Nabucco. Renata Scotto, Matteo Manuguerra, Nicolai Ghiaurov, Veriano Luchetti, Elena Obraztsova, Robert Lloyd, Kenneth Collins, Anne Edwards. Ambrosian Opera Chorus and Boys' Chorus, National Philharmonic Orch., Riccardo Muti, cond. *RCA CRL3-2951.*

Otello. Renata Scotto, Plácido Domingo, Sherrill Milnes, Frank Little, Paul Crook, Paul Plishka, Malcolm King, Jean Kraft; Ambrosian Opera Chorus, National Philharmonic Orch., James Levine, cond. *RCA CRL 3-2951.*

Rigoletto. Renata Scotto, Alfredo Kraus, Ettore Bastianini, Ivo Vinco, Fiorenza Cossotto. Gianandrea Gavazzeni, cond. Maggio Musicale Fiorentino. *Ricordi AOCL-316003; Mercury SR3-9012.*

Rigoletto. Renata Scotto, Carlo Bergonzi, Dietrich Fischer-Dieskau, Fiorenza Cossotto, Ivo Vinco, Piero de Palma, Mirella Fiorentini, Lorenzo Testi, Virgilio Carbonari, Catarina Alda, Giuseppe Morresi. La Scala Chorus and Orch., Rafael Kubelik, cond. *DG 2709014.*

Rigoletto. Renata Scotto, Kostas Paskalis; Vienna State Opera, 1960 (?), Carlo Maria Giulini, cond. (live, uncredited) *HOPE* (UK).

Rigoletto. Renata Scotto, Richard Tucker, Cornell MacNeil, William Wilderman. Fernando Previtale, cond. Teatro Colón, 1967 (live). *HRE269-2.*

Rigoletto. Renata Scotto, Piero Cappuccilli. Carlo Franci (?) cond. Metropolitan Opera (?), 1970 (live, uncredited). *HRE-V 816-2.*

La Traviata. Renata Scotto, Gianni Raimondi, Ettore Bastianini, Giuliana Tavolaccini, Armanda Bonato, Franco Ricciardi, Giuseppe Morresi, Virgilio Carbonari, Silvio Maionica, Angelo Mercuriali. La Scala Chorus and Orch., Antonino Votto, cond. *DG 2726049.*

La Traviata. Renata Scotto, Alfredo Kraus, Renato Bruson, Sarah Walker, Cynthia Buchan, Henry Newman, Richard Van Allan, Roderick Kennedy, Suso Mariátegui, Max-Rene Cosotti, Christopher Keyte. Ambrosian Opera Chorus, The Band of Her Majesty's Royal Marines, Philharmonia Orch., Riccardo Muti, cond. *EMI 1C 165-43127/29* (German News); *Angel DSX-3920.*

I vespri siciliani. Renata Scotto, Veriano Luchetti, Ruggero Raimondi, Carlo del Bosco, Graziano Polidori, Gianpaolo Corradi, Gianfranco Manganotti, Giorgio Giorgetti, Carlo Novelli. Riccardo Muti, cond. Maggio Musicale Fiorentino, May 13, 1978. *Legendary Recordings LR 169-4.*

Scotto began her career with Verdi, first auditioning at the age of fourteen with *"Stride la vampa!"* later making her debut as Violetta at the age of eighteen. She has been well represented on records in the Verdi repertory, and her growth as an artist and a Verdian may be traced through these records. The first *Traviata* under Votto is an example of the best of the Italian tradition of performance until recent times; the second under Muti, Votto's protégé, illustrates the growth and refinement of that tradition. Both are conducted by great Verdians, part of a line that can be traced through Votto to Toscanini to Verdi himself. The first one finds Scotto as a brilliant coloratura soprano in the first act, interpolating high notes wherever possible and extending cadenzas with the desperate abandon of Verdi's demimondaine herself. The performance has what came to be accepted as standard cuts, much freedom is taken with rhythm, and it sounds like the best one might expect in a good Italian theater. Muti's *Traviata* is note-complete, and the maestro's insistence on following the letter of the score has a revelatory effect on the music; by now Scotto has learned not to add to what Verdi wrote but to find all possible meanings within the composer's intentions. It is arguably her finest Verdi recording, perhaps even the best of all her recordings, with close competition from her *Butterfly*.

Rigoletto was also recorded twice in the studio, and the two recordings are quite different in another way. Bastianini is the more Italianate protagonist, Fischer-Dieskau the most controversial. Gavazzeni certainly is idiomatic, powerful, *contadino;* and Kubelik is none of those things. Yet both records work and work very well, in fact the DG set earned Scotto a Grand Prix du Disque when it was released in Europe. Scotto's Gilda is one of a long series of heroines to which Scotto restored femininity: she is no silver-voiced music machine, she is a woman. The aria *"Caro nome"* is sung in both sets not as a display of virtuosity but as a simple paean to a young girl's first love. The 1960 Gavazzeni recording, with Kraus and Bastianini, is still one of the best available and easily the most authentic. The Kubelik set, however, finds Scotto unwittingly singing even more carefully, perhaps spurred into it by Fischer-Dieskau's obsessive fastidiousness; and she manages to find the dramatic truth and remain faithful to her Verdian roots. She has never sung *"Caro nome"* more carefully or affectingly than in this recording, and the virtuosity of her first scene with Rigoletto has not been equaled. One HRE set is labeled Buenos Aires but more likely both are from the Met; the 1967 record is representative of Scotto's portrayal of Gilda, but neither she nor Tucker is in the best voice and the sound is quite poor. The Cappuccilli-Scotto pairing on HRE provides some of each singer's most uninhibited and thrilling singing on records.

I vespri siciliani is too good a recording to be called a pirate. The performance at this Maggio Musicale is simply the best on records, as well as the most complete. Muti, always better in the theater than in the studio, is at his Verdian best here; and his collaboration with Scotto is as fruitful as it was in the *Traviata* recording. From the opening recitative, *"O mio fratel . . . morte al tiran"* through the final scene there is inner logic to the soprano's creation within this vast panoramic work. The two artists are good for each other: Scotto is kept musically on her toes while the drama is only heightened; Muti is made more flexible for her than for any other singer. The entire cast is in the best of voices, and the recorded sound is excellent. This document of one of the finest Verdi performances of our time cannot be recommended too highly.

The *Ballo* recordings stem from the series of Chicago performances that followed in the wake of the infamous San Francisco *Gioconda*, with the same principals; the atmosphere was not the most conducive to the best artistic results, although Scotto's Amelia deserves to be recorded. The recording of the complete performance was suppressed by HRE for fear of litigation; the highlights record on Legendary Recordings is coupled with *Macbeth* scenes.

I Lombardi also is available on private recordings, and

the 1969 Rome performance was a turning point in Scotto's career; it is a beautiful souvenir, with adequate sound.
The later New York concert performance reveals some
pitch problems for both Scotto and Carreras in the beginning, but it sizzles by the end of the opera.

Nabucco is an opera that Scotto has never done onstage
and is not interested in doing; she was talked into the recording by Muti. Judging from the fire audible in her
reading, it is probably a good thing that it was Muti who
led the musical forces, since she is always on the thrilling
edge of going overboard. Still, the character of Abigaille is
too one-dimensional for Scotto's gifts, and the best moments in the record are purely musical: *"Anch'io dischiuso
. . ."* is a bel canto scene, never vulgar or veristic despite
some severe attempts at chest notes. Muti is more martial
than moving, but there is undeniable drive in this recording.

Otello is one of the great Verdi records. The combination of Scotto, Domingo, Milnes, and Levine shows the
Met forces at their best (it is a crime that Levine could not
use his own Met Orchestra for the recording, for under
him those musicians have few rivals). It was done in very
long takes, and the excitement of the stage is captured
quite well. Scotto is simply the most Italian, the most Verdian of Desdemonas of our time. Verdi's Desdemona was
much more of a woman than Shakespeare's, and Act IV of
this record recreates the magic of Scotto's first Desdemona
at the Met—she is all Verdian femininity.

The Verdi *Requiem* finds Scotto again musically pre-
cise and devastatingly human; the *"Libera me"* is an outcry
of dignity and rage that never strays from Verdi's nota-
tion. The women are superior to the men in this recording, but all are driven to superhuman efforts by Muti.

Scotto shapes phrases with a deep feeling equaled only by her miraculous *Traviata*, a Verdian performance of the highest order. As with *Traviata*, the EMI-Electrola pressings (available in this country through German News Co.) are superior to the domestic Angel pressings.

Macbeth gave Scotto one of her greatest roles, and the Ravinia off-the-air recording is indispensable until she records the opera in the studio. The Chicago forces are without equal, and Levine's conducting is awesome in its power. Scotto's voice sounded thicker this summer than it did in the same role in the following two seasons; *"La luce langue,"* in particular, is more musical in this concert performance than it has been onstage; but the phrase *"è necessario,"* for example, carries a frightening descent into chest voice that makes this character truly terrifying. The sound is quite good. The HRE recording will remain a treasure even after Scotto has recorded her Lady Macbeth commercially. The Covent Garden performance, available only in highlights, is fascinating but still not fully formed: Muti's excitement carries the evening, but many details remain musical problems solved rather than the dramatic inventions they would become in two short seasons: the recitatives, the articulation of words like *"requiem"* and *"eternità"* in *"La luce langue"* all are better integrated in the drama in the Chicago recording and all point to Scotto's growth in what has become one of her best roles.

ERMANNO WOLF-FERRARI (1876–1948)

Il segretto di Susanna. Renata Scotto, Renato Bruson. Philharmonia Orch., John Pritchard, cond. *CBS 1M-36733.*

This is not a musical challenge for either Scotto or Bruson, but it certainly is a comic triumph. In the smoking Countess, Scotto found an agreeable change of pace from all her tragic heroines and the record sounds as if she had not enjoyed herself so much since the days of *La Serva Padrona*.

MISCELLANEOUS RECITALS

A Portrait of Renata Scotto. Rossini: *"Una voce poco fa."* Bellini: *"Qui la voce . . . Vien, diletto."* Puccini: *"O mio babbino caro"*; *"Signore, ascolta"*; *"Tu che di gel sei cinto"*; *"Un bel dì"*; *"Con onor muore"*. Donizetti: *"Il dolce suono . . . Spargi d'amaro pianto."* Verdi: *"È' strano . . . Sempre libera."* Philharmonia Orch., Manno Wolf-Ferrari and Sir John Barbirolli, conds. *EMI ASD 4022.*

Renata Scotto: Arie di Bellini. *"Oh, quante volte"*; *"Qui la voce"*; *"Prendi, l'anel ti dono"*; *"Ah! non credea mirarti"*; *"Vaga luna, che inargenti."* With Giuseppe Baratti, tenor. Sicilian Symphony Orch, Ottavio Ziino, cond. Teatro Massimo, Catania, June 3, 1961 (live). *Fonit-Cetra DOC 39.*

Renata Scotto: Arias by Puccini, Mascagni, Cilèa, Catalani. Columbia M-33435.

Renata Scotto: Respighi. Il Tramonto, with the Tokyo String Quartet; Ten songs, including *"Deità silvane,"* Thomas Fulton, piano. *Vox Cum Laude VCL-9039(D).*

Renata Scotto Sings Verdi. Arias from *La Traviata, Otello, Nabucco, I Lombardi, I Vespri Siciliani, La Battaglia di*

Legnano. London Philharmonic Orch., Gianandrea Gavazzeni, cond. *Columbia M 33516.*

Renata Scotto: Serenata. Songs by Puccini, Leoncavallo, Mascagni, Catalani, Pizzetti, Respighi, Wolf-Ferrari. John Atkins, piano. *Columbia M 34501.*

Renata Scotto: Songs by Rossini, Bellini, Donizetti, Verdi. Including the *Giovanna d'Arco* cantata. Walter Baracchi, piano. *RCA AGL-1341.*

Renata Scotto: The Art of Bel Canto. Scenes from *Armida* and *Anna Bolena* Eve Queler, cond. (live, uncredited; 1975); and from *Il Pirata* and *Medea* Lorin Maazel, cond. (live, uncredited; 1979) *Legendary Recordings LR-108.*

Mirella Freni and Renata Scotto. Duets by Mozart, Mercadante, and Bellini. National Philharmonic Orch., Lorenzo Anselmi and Leone Magiera, conds. *London OS-26652*

Monte Carlo Opera Gala. Arias from *Linda di Chamounix, I Puritani,* and *Aida;* with orchestral selections from *Norma, William Tell,* and *I Vespri Siciliani.* Monte Carlo Opera Orchestra, Louis Frémaux, cond. *DG SLPM 138 653.*

Renata Scotto and Plácido Domingo: Romantic Duets. From *Manon, Roméo et Juliette, Fedora, I Rantzau.* National Philharmonic Orch., Kurt Herbert Adler, cond. *Columbia M 35135.*

Renata Scotto and José Carreras: Great Operatic Scenes. From *I Lombardi* (1972); *La Traviata* (1973); *Madama Butterfly* (1974); *La Bohème* (1977); *Adriana Lecouvreur* (1978).

(live uncredited: New York, Tokyo, San Francisco, and New York, respectively). *HRE-351-2.*

La Scala at the Bolshoi. Renata Scotto gala concert at Tchaikovsky Hall (live, 1964). *"O quante volte"*; *"Ah! non credea mirarti . . . Ah! non giunge"*; *"Prendi, per me sei libero"*; *"Addio del passato"*; *"Caro nome"*; *"Ah, fors'e lui . . . Sempre libera."* Antonio Tonini, piano. Included in set with joint concert by Mirella Freni, Birgit Nilsson, Fiorenza Cossotto, and Bruno Prevedi; and scenes from *Il Trovatore*, *La Bohème*, and *Turandot*; does not include the Scotto *Lucia di Lammermoor* at the Bolshoi. *HRE-340-5.*

Christmas with Renata Scotto at St. Patrick's Cathedral. Lorenzo Anselmi, cond. *"Les Anges dans Nos Campagnes"*; "He Shall Feed His Flock"; *"Tu Scendi dalle Stelle"*; "Joy to the World"; "Silent Night"; *"Ave Maria"*; "Christmas at the Cloisters"; "Adeste Fideles"; *Panis Angelicus;* *"Ave Maria"*; "What Child Is This?"; "Lully, Lullay"; "Mariä Wiegenlied"; *"Cantique de Noël"*. *RCA ARL1-4136.*

Verdi Gala (anthology): *"Addio del passato,"* from a RAI-Torino broadcast, Arturo Basile, cond. *Acanta 23.519.*

Renata Scotto Live in Paris. Ivan Davis, piano. Handel: *"Lascia ch'io pianga"*; Scarlatti: *"Cara e dolce"*; *"Bellezza, che s'ama"*; Rossini: *Soirées Musicales* (selections); Liszt: Three Petrarch sonnets; Verdi: *"La preghiera del poeta"*; *"Il brigidin"*; *"Pietà, signore"*; *Stornello;* Puccini: *"Storiella d'amore"*; *"D'ogni dolor"*; Respighi: *"Soupir"*; *"Au milieu du jardin"*; Mascagni: *"Senti, bambino"*; *"Perchè dovrei temare?"*; *"M'ama, non m'ama"*; Puccini: *"Vissi d'arte."* Recorded live on

March 28, 1983, at the Théâtre de l'Athénée. *Etcet-era ETC 2002 (Qualiton Imports).*

Renata Scotto and Giulietta Simionato. Orchestra Lirica della Cetra, Corrado Benvenuti and Arturo Basile, conds. Bellini: *"Come per me sereno";* Donizetti: *"Quel guardo il cavalier";* Verdi: *"Amami, Alfredo"; "Addio del passato";* Bizet: *"Siccome un dì";* Mascagni: *"Flammen perdonammi."* Side 2 includes Simionato in arias by Rossini, Cimarosa, Verdi, and Mascagni. *Fonit-Cetra (PSI) LPO 2077.*

Renata Scotto canta arie di Rossini, Cherubini, Verdi, Pergolesi, Donizetti. I Virtuosi di Roma, Renato Fasano, cond.; La Scala Orch., Tullio Serafin and Nino Sonzogno, conds.; Maggio Musicale Fiorentino, Gianandrea Gavazzeni, cond. Rossini: *"Vorrei spiegarvi il giubilo";* Cherubini: *"O Amore, vieni a me";* Verdi: *"Gualtier Maldè . . . Caro nome"; "Tutte le feste al tempio"; "Solo per me l'infamia";* Pergolesi: *"Stizzoso, mio stizzoso"; "A Serpina penserete";* Donizetti: *"Regnava nel silenzio"; "Quando rapito in estasi"; "Ardon gli incensi"; "Spargi d'amaro pianto."* Ricordi-Orizzonte *(PSI) OCL 16155.*

Great Artists at the Met: Renata Scotto. Rome Opera, Sir John Barbirolli, cond.; La Scala Orch., Antonino Votto and Rafael Kubelik, conds.; National Philharmonic Orch., James Levine and Lorenzo Anselmi, conds.; London Symphony Orch., Gianandrea Gavazzeni, cond. Puccini: *"Un bel dì"; "Con onor muore"; "Mi chiamano Mimì"; "Donde lieta uscì";* Musetta's Waltz; Verdi: *"Addio del passato"; "Caro nome"; "Salce, salce . . . Ave Maria";* Bellini: *"Mira, O Norma"* (with Mirella Freni). *Metropolitan Opera Guild R71.*

Met Stars on Broadway. Renata Scotto sings Stephen Sondheim's "Send in the Clowns" from *A Little Night Music,* Lorenzo Anselmi, cond. Also includes Broadway selections by Ezio Pinza, Leontyne Price, Robert Weede, Risë Stevens, Cesare Siepi, Renata Tebaldi, Roberta Peters, Eileen Farrell, Giulietta Simionato, Ettore Bastianini, Dorothy Kirsten, Birgit Nilsson. *Metropolitan Opera Guild MET 204.*

Two Mezzo-soprano Arias. Renata Scotto with Emilio Ghirardini, piano. Ponchielli: *"Voce di donna";* Verdi: *"Stride la vampa."* Live private recording, Milan, 1950. (Awaiting release).

Renata Scotto Verdi Arias. Scenes and Arias from *Don Carlo, Ernani, Macbeth, I Masnadieri, Un ballo in maschera,* and *Aida.* Hungarian State Opera Orch., Thomas Fulton, cond. *Hungaroton-Qualiton* (Awaiting release).

In recitals, Scotto has said, she becomes most herself, exposed and totally given to her audience. Her very first recital, the EMI *Portrait of Renata Scotto,* finds a young and promising singer in beautiful voice but without the finish she would acquire in a few short seasons; that is, with the exception of a carefully sung and very moving *"Vien, diletto,"* where she avoids the interpolated high E-flat at the close and stays close to the score and to the heart of Elvira. Her Sicilian recital *Arie di Bellini* finds her taking every high option possible, on the other hand, and the *"Vien, diletto"* from *I Puritani* in that recording ranks with some of her loveliest Bellini singing on records. Both reveal the womanly sound that has been her trademark through all periods of her development, with a particularly sexy *"Una voce poco fa"* in the EMI album. *"Ah! non credea mirarti"* is ravishing in the Sicilian recording, but it is even better in the famed Bolshoi recital, one pirate record worth finding (once available in the Soviet Union on Melodiya). The Verdi and verismo albums contain much music that would only later enter her stage repertory, and they are beautiful illustrations of the valid differences between singing an aria in character in context and interpreting out of context without betraying its origin. The recent Respighi recital finds Scotto competing for sheer instrumental beauty with the Tokyo String Quartet, and all five musicians are at their most expressive in the haunting *Il Tramonto. Serenata* is her first recital recorded in the United States and finds her supported by her most sensitive accompanist, John Atkins. The *Monte Carlo Gala* teases with a surprisingly stentorian *"Qui Radames verrà . . . O patria mia"* and a veiled and very lovely *"Son vergin vezzosa."* Scotto's Christmas album is a work of love and a joyous triumph conducted by her husband, Lorenzo Anselmi; in particular Franck's *Panis Angelicus* is at once pleading and serene, religious fervor at its finest musical expression; Corigliano's "Christmas at the Cloisters" catches Scotto at a rare moment of rhythmic imprecision but is a thrilling glimpse at what this instrument could do in the contemporary repertory. The conductor obviously loves his singer, and the whole affair is festive and peaceful, a Christmas album for every season. Likewise the duet album with Mirella Freni, also conducted by Anselmi (whose total conducting credits were mislabeled on the album); the two singers are quite different in temperament but surprisingly alike in timbre, and the vocal blend is particularly gratifying in the *Norma* duet. Anselmi's conducting of this duet in particular suggests that perhaps he should be doing much more of this type of work. The RCA recital of songs by Rossini, Bellini, Donizetti, and Verdi contains the *Giovanna d'Arco* cantata already discussed as well as many treasures from the singer's preferred composers; this more than any other studio recital album captures the spontaneity, or its magical illusion, that Scotto brings to the live recital stage. The Domingo duet album with Kurt Herbert Adler conducting is a souvenir of a great stage partnership and more: *Fedora* pages provide a preview of something that should happen for Scotto; the *Manon "Toi! Vous!"* shows that she is quite ready to return to the French *Manon* with renewed force after Puccini. And the duet from *I Rantzau* makes a case for a major Mascagni revival. Despite bland conducting, the singing is thrilling. Thrilling also is the occasion of a Scotto and Carreras pairing, and the HRE set has compiled all that can be compiled on that account. The *Traviata* has Carreras as a last-minute substitute in Japan in 1973, and the scenes are vigorous and stylish; the *Butterfly* is probably from San Francisco (1974), and the *Bohème* is the Met's from 1977 in a particularly affecting performance. *Adriana* is bettered only by the commercial recording, and that only because of the sound quality since this is some of each singer's very best dramatic singing. Unfortunately not all the selections have been pressed at the correct pitch in this set. Pitch is also a problem in the pirate *Art of Bel Canto*, which compiles performances under Eve Queler and Lorin Maazel; the singing is very good, with a clever recovery from an early entrance in the *Armida* selection, but with poor sound throughout. *Renata Scotto Sings Verdi* is a lesson in that composer's sensibility. It is particularly interesting to notice that in *"Addio del pas-*

sato, " with Gavazzeni conducting, Scotto is already much more faithful to the letter of the score than she had been years earlier, and that the miracle of the Muti *Traviata,* as well as the Levine *Otello,* had been brewing in the soprano's mind for some time.

The Cetra recital album was originally paired with a side of arias by the soprano Magda Olivero which is now out of print; the present coupling with Simionato makes for a very fine package. On the Scotto side, *"Siccome un dì"* alone is reason enough for this re-release: it is from Bizet's *I pescatori di perle,* with which the soprano had great success in the 1950s but from which she recorded nothing except this aria. The technique is sweetly exposed, with the tone slightly covered on top and veiled through the soft palate to produce a haunting sound. The same is true of Bellini's *"Come per me sereno,"* although here there is rhythmic carelessness and a surprisingly generalized characterization. The unusual selections from *La Traviata,* *"Amami, Alfredo"* and the spoken reading of Germont's letter preceding *"Addio del passato,"* attest to the acclaim that the young soprano had received early on as an actress as well as a singer. The aria from *Don Pasquale* is the same audition piece that won Scotto the leading role in Menotti's *Amelia al ballo* for her first Cairo season; it is picaresque and bright, complete with a very naughty peal of laughter at the center. The forthcoming Hungaroton Verdi album contains among other things indispensable souvenirs or roles the soprano has sung at the Met but not recorded complete: *"Non pianger, mia compagna"* and *"Tu che le vanità"* from Verdi's *Don Carlo;* and *"La luce langue"* as well as the Sleepwalking Scene from Verdi's *Macbeth.* Another beautiful souvenir is the Metropolitan Opera Guild's *Great Artists at the Met* album; although all of the selections have been previously released, the juxtaposition of roles is enlightening, with Mimi followed by her friend Musetta, and Desdemona followed by Norma. The other Met album, *Met Stars on Broadway,* is a treasure. Scotto's contribution was recorded especially for this album and is not available anywhere else: "Send in the Clowns," a favorite concert encore of the soprano in an arrangement by Anthony Meloni that rivals Jonathan Tunick's original and Lorenzo Anselmi conducting. There is mature melancholy from the first "Isn't it rich . . . ?" with dark and sensuous colors in the voice and a discreet *parlando* insinuated in "quick, send in the clowns" and again in "well, maybe next year." Sondheim's idiom is simple, but the soprano knows how to bring out its profound beauty.

The tapes from Renata Scotto's 1950 rendering of two mezzo arias with her teacher at the piano had been lost for years and have been found only recently. They are sound images of youth, of energy and talent untrained but unstoppable. And they celebrate thirty-five years of recordings.

Select List of
Performances on Videotape

DONIZETTI: *Lucia di Lammermoor*. Renata Scotto, Carlo Bergonzi, Mario Zanasi, Plinio Clabassi. Bruno Bartoletti, cond. Tokyo, March 9, 1967.

GOUNOD: *Faust*. Renata Scotto, Alfredo Kraus, Nicolai Ghiaurov, Lorenzo Saccomani. Paul Ethuin, cond. Tokyo, September 9, 1973.

PONCHIELLI: *La Gioconda*. Renata Scotto, Stefania Toczyska, Norman Mittelman, Ferruccio Furlanetto. Bruno Bartoletti, cond. San Francisco Opera, September 1979.

PUCCINI: *La Bohème*. Renata Scotto (as Mimi), Maralin Niska, Ingvar Wixell, Paul Plishka. James Levine, cond. Metropolitan Opera, March 15, 1977.

PUCCINI: *La Bohème*. Renata Scotto (as Musetta), Teresa Stratas, José Carreras, Richard Stilwell, James Morris. James Levine, cond. Metropolitan Opera, January 16, 1982.

PUCCINI: *Manon Lescaut*. Renata Scotto, Plácido Domingo, Pablo Elvira, Renato Capecchi. James Levine, cond. Metropolitan Opera, March 29, 1980.

PUCCINI: *Il Trittico*. Renata Scotto, Cornell MacNeil, Vasile Moldoveanu, Bianca Berini, Italo Tajo, Jocelyne Taillon, Betsy Norden, Gabriel Bacquier, Philip Creech. James Levine, cond. Metropolitan Opera, November 14, 1981.

VERDI: *Don Carlo*. Renata Scotto, Vasile Moldoveanu, Tatiana Troyanos, Sherrill Milnes, Paul Plishka. James Levine, cond. Metropolitan Opera, February 21, 1980.

VERDI: *Luisa Miller*. Renata Scotto, Plácido Domingo, Sherrill Milnes, Bonaldo Giaiotti, James Morris, Jean Kraft. James Levine, cond. Metropolitan Opera, January 20, 1979.

VERDI: *Otello*. Renata Scotto, Jon Vickers, Cornell Mac-Neil. James Levine, cond. Metropolitan Opera, September 25, 1978.

VERDI: *La Traviata*. Renata Scotto, José Carreras, Sesto Bruscantini. Nino Verchi, cond. Tokyo, September 19, 1973.

ZANDONAI: *Francesca da Rimini*. Renata Scotto, Plácido Domingo, Cornell MacNeil, William Lewis, Isola Jones. James Levine, cond. Metropolitan Opera (scheduled for telecast 1984–85).

CONCERTS:

Beverly Sills's Farewell Performance (1980).

Renata Scotto and Plácido Domingo in San Juan (1980).

United Nations Day Concert (with Jon Vickers, 1981).

PBS *Gala of Stars* (1982–84).

Renata Scotto in Concert in Caracas (1983).

Tribute to Maria Callas (Chicago, 1983).

NON-SINGING APPEARANCES:

Callas (1978).

"The Making of An Opera: "La Gioconda" (San Francisco, September 1979).

Portrait of a Prima Donna (Houston, 1979).

Metropolitan Opera Centennial Gala (1983).

Acknowledgments

This book was written offstage and on the road. Many people helped. First thanks must go to our families, whose patience and encouragement made these three years very enjoyable. Louise Gault, our editor at Doubleday, offered us not only her support but also friendship worthy of Verdi's Marquis of Posa. Special acknowledgments must go to the many friends and colleagues mentioned in the text whose stories intersect the one we have told and who have done much to create its substance: in particular Jonathan Pell, for suggesting the idea of the book and for introducing the two authors; Susan F. Schulman and Robert Lombardo, for splendid support well beyond the call of duty or even of friendship; and Ernest Gilbert. The discography owes its thoroughness to the generous assistance of our friend Howard Hart, who should also be thanked for his kindness and hospitality along with Michael Rosen, John Miller, and Mark Lameier; Carol Cates, John Atkins; Peter Fay and the staff of the Kennedy Center's Performing Arts Library in Washington, D.C.; Gretchen Feltes, Cynthia Arkin, Ricardo Palomares, Paul Hume, Meg Mc-Court, and Gary Burget.

Index